Published by Semiotext(e)
PO Box 629, South Pasadena, CA 91031
www.semiotexte.com

Cover photograph: Kevin Dietsch, *Allen & Company Annual Conference Draws Media and Tech Leaders to Sun Valley*

Design: Hedi El Kholti
ISBN: 978-1-63590-268-6

10 9 8 7 6 5 4 3 2 1

Distributed by the MIT Press, Cambridge, MA, and London, England
Printed and bound in the United States of America

LAST WEEK IN END TIMES CINEMA

A. S. Hamrah

Semiotext(e)

CONTENTS

March 17, 2024

Absurd awards-show irritant Billy Porter to cowrite and star in James Baldwin biopic

Civil War director Alex Garland announces he can't choose sides, can't tell good from bad

Flamin' Hot director Eva Longoria awarded $50 million Bezos grant

Netflix Lindsay Lohan starrer *Irish Wish* is new low in found object/crap moviemaking

March 24, 2024

Big-budget Hollywood *Cola Wars* movie will dramatize 1980s and '90s Coke & Pepsi market share struggle that captured the imagination of no one

Actor Aaron Taylor-Johnson, star of superhero movies, franchise movies, and sequels, says, "We've all had enough of seeing certain studio films, a certain kind of pop culture," then signs up to do more of same

Sylvester Stallone given Ruth Bader Ginsburg Award; ceremony canceled on account of that's stupid

Runaway Train director Andrei Konchalovsky calls Russian presidential election freest and fairest and most democratic in the entire world

"Jake Gyllenhaal in *Road House* on Amazon"

March 31, 2024

Major Disney shareholder 81-year-old Nelson Peltz opposes studio making films starring Black people and/or women

Very successful screenwriter Steven Zaillian, age 71, thinks all movies in 1955 were in black-and-white

Mass staff exodus at Hot Docs in Toronto as fest flounders under guidance of leaders Marie Nelson and Hussain Currimbhoy

Facebook allowed Netflix to read Facebook users' DMs; closed their streaming service to please Netflix, a top advertiser

Mark Wahlberg admits two films he starred in sucked: the Tim Burton *Planet of the Apes* remake and Jonathan Demme *Charade* remake

Night of the Hunter remake coming from superhero/horror director Scott Derrickson, who is no Charles Laughton

April 7, 2024

Wealthy eyebrowless OpenAI honcho Sam Altman declares that cinema will become video games, which in turn will become "unimaginably great"

This year's International Short Film Fest Oberhausen in turmoil over head Lars Henrik Gass's anti-Palestinian policies

Ken Loach will retire after 36 feature films in 60 years on the right side of history; Alex Garland also says he's retiring

Human Rights Watch Film Fest will end operation this year

Dune: Part Two doing great at box office, but will be moved to streaming in bid by WBD to increase Max subs

Serbian director Emir Kusturica visits Putin in Kremlin for public ass-kissing session

April 14, 2024

Netflix won't produce David Lynch's animated movie

Studios make it very clear they will not distribute Francis Ford Coppola's *Megalopolis*

Theater owners beg studios to make nonblockbuster mid-budget fare

Benny Safdie bands with ridiculous cop Mayor Eric Adams to solve big NYC problem: composting

Nicola Peltz Beckham, daughter of billionaire racist-sexist Disney investor & daughter-in-law of Beckhams, directs her first feature, *Lola*, about young woman living in poverty

Irritating, unfunny voice actor Josh Gad to direct Chris Farley biopic

April 21, 2024

Articles in *Harper's* and *Lit Hub* declare that all forms of writing, from poetry to screenwriting, are now professionally untenable

Mandate of new Netflix film production head, Dan Lin, is: Make fewer, cheaper, even worse movies. Or something like that. Netflix CEO Ted Sarandos keeps changing it in press interviews. It may be: Make same amount of films, just as good as ones they've already made. No, better. But definitely cheaper. And no auteurs

Netflix adding AI images of suspects to true crime shows

Netflix will no longer report subscription numbers

Trailer debuts for first all-AI movie, *Next Stop Paris*, a romance for TLC television from producer of *Sharknado* movies

Do-gooder boutique studio Participant goes bust, lays off staff of 100, closes; were producers of good movies: *Fast Food Nation*, *Dark Waters*, *All the Beauty and the Bloodshed*; cringe items / Oscar bait: *An Inconvenient Truth*, *The Help*, *Green Book*; many more in-between

WBD CEO David Zaslav gets a 26.5% raise to $49.7 million after studio loses over $3 billion in 2023. WBD stock price down 66% since he took over; studio remains over $40 billion in debt

Trump's Truth Social will add streaming service to show "films that have been canceled"

The house of Bollywood star Salman Khan shot up by Bishnoi gang, part of sect opposed to Khan's antelope hunting. Khan remains unpunished for killing a homeless man in 2002 hit-and-run, blaming it on his chauffeur

Strange conservative website *Quillette* publishes philistine two-part takedown of Jean-Luc Godard that is error ridden and bonkers

Max Azzarello, manifesto writer who died after setting himself on fire in front of NYC courthouse where Trump is on trial, previously hosted podcast about Laura Dern called *Dern After Reading*

Liam Neeson and Pamela Anderson to star in *Naked Gun* remake

April 28, 2024

Selling point of *Deadpool & Wolverine* is that it doesn't require any "Marvel homework"

WBD and Amazon "may have unknowingly" used North Korean companies for animation work on two of their TV series

Studios have begun hiring some directors based on the Rotten Tomatoes scores of their recent movies

Kalshi, a financial exchange and predictive-market company, offers a betting product for Rotten Tomatoes scores. "Now anyone can make money by being a movie critic," is how they sell it

WBD CEO David Zaslav's $49.7 million salary is more than the entire operating budget of WBD's Turner Classic Movies, flagship channel of American film history

Instead of reporting subscriber numbers, Netflix will use a new metric they call "Fandom," which is based on how many people watch trailers or parts of trailers on their platform. "Over six billion impressions every month," they claim, as if that means anything

Comedian–*Unfrosted* director Jerry Seinfeld says "the movie business is over," replaced by "depression, malaise, confusion—

disorientation." This succinct, not untrue statement has got him mocked on social media

Jean-Luc Godard's last film, *Scénarios*, completed the day before he died, will debut at Cannes, then be distributed and sold by an NFT company, Roadstead

Rapper-director Kanye West launching adult entertainment studio, Yeezy Porn

Writer-director Aaron Sorkin is planning an antidisinformation J6 movie that is also a sequel to *The Social Network*

Jurassic World: Fallen Kingdom star Chris Pratt and wife Katherine Schwarzenegger, author of the book *The Gift of Forgiveness: Inspiring Stories from Those Who Have Overcome the Unforgivable*, have torn down the architecturally significant modernist Zimmerman House in Brentwood, built 1950. The couple purchased the house for $12.5 million and will replace it with a 15,000-square-foot "modern farmhouse"–style mansion

A saggy, older, deflated appearance is characteristic of the emaciation now known in Hollywood as "Ozempic face," named after the prescription weight-loss drug that's overprescribed in Los Angeles. Using too much of it too quickly is causing an endemic zombielike look, with sunken eyes and gaunt cheeks

Things Change writer-director David Mamet insists his two actor daughters, Zosia and Clara, are not nepo babies, because learning from being on set earned them a spot in the bigs. "They haven't benefited from any type of privilege," he says

Writer-director-actor Ben Stiller announces he was shocked no one liked *Zoolander 2*. The comedy sequel came out in 2016

Lucasfilm has partnered with a dairy company to make and sell *Star Wars* Blue Milk. Formerly only available at Disney theme parks, the liquid food product will be sold in grocery stores and through DoorDash

Tram derails at Universal Studios Hollywood as it passes too quickly through the *Jurassic Park* exhibit. Fifteen injured, some seriously. California Highway Patrol investigating

May 5, 2024

May the fifth be with you

Shocking *Mufasa: The Lion King* reveal: it features new songs by Lin-Manuel Miranda

Paramount Global replaces CEO with tripartite hydra-headed arrangement: each of the three new men was introduced during an earnings call by playing a recording of the *Mission: Impossible* theme—music from a movie the studio claims flopped last year despite doubling its $291 million budget at the box office

Bain Capital will build a movie-soundstage complex in Red Hook, Brooklyn. A previous plan of theirs to build a film studio in Sunset Park fell through, possibly because it was supposed to include affordable housing

Peacock will hike their streaming subscription price $2 before the Olympics begin. The Olympics were previously shown on broadcast television for free, starting in 1960

CEO Anthony Wood says Roku will begin showing video ads on the Roku home screen

Dwayne "The Rock" Johnson is often eight hours late to the set of *Red One*, an Amazon MGM movie "audiences are going to love this holiday season." The Christmas movie has cost the studio over $250 million so far

Miller's Girl (terrible title) came and went in theaters in January. Now it's a top Netflix movie, dark story of romance between pixie-sprite gothgirl Jenna Ortega, 21, and gray-haired British character actor and hobbit Martin Freeman, 52. Defending the film, Freeman mentioned that Liam Neeson had done a Holocaust movie

Apple TV+ says garbage theatrical flop *Argylle* is a big hit now that it's on their platform; Apple also produced the film

Apple TV+ series *Sugar* stars Colin Farrell as an alien (or something) who identifies with 1940s film noir. Thus the show, according to *Entertainment Weekly*, which is not a weekly, "continually references classic noir films starring Humphrey Bogart and Robert Mitchum" with "constant shoutouts to old Hollywood, which are often visualized via brief cutaways to actual footage from the movies"

Ryan Gosling will ditch dark roles, concentrate on films he thinks are good for his family to see. The actor-director says he was aligned with his daughters when he appeared in *Barbie* because they "were already making little movies about Barbie on the iPad"

Marvel star Chris Hemsworth admits that *Thor: Love and Thunder* was "a whiff" in which the Australian actor "became a parody of himself"

British musician FKA twigs testified before a US Senate subcommittee that though she is opposed to deepfake AIs, she has created one of herself to make her social media appearances for her

Country music star Randy Travis, who had a debilitating stroke eleven years ago, has released a new single featuring an AI version of his voice

Source of "Everyone Knows That," viral lostwave music phenomenon, turns out to be 1986 porn film *Angels of Passion*

Airbnb offering "Icons" rentals based on movies including *Up*, *Purple Rain*, *X-Men*, and forthcoming *Inside Out 2*. "Icons take you into worlds that only exist in your imagination," says Airbnb cofounder Brian Chesky. "As life becomes increasingly digital, we're focused on bringing more magic into the real world [and] we've created the most extraordinary experiences on Earth"

When Robert De Niro was caught in the streets of New York shouting "This is not a movie!" he was not yelling at pro-Palestinian protesters, as some had assumed. The *Mean Streets* actor was shooting a scene on location for his first TV series, for Netflix

May 12, 2024

Upholstered in rich Corinthian leather, *Thor: Love and Thunder* director Taika Waititi dressed as a recliner to attend the Met Gala in New York

Apple released a TV commercial / crush video in which all the music and art of the world is smashed and compressed by a giant trash compactor into their worthless new, thinner iPad

The public reacted to the Apple ad spot with overwhelming disgust, so Apple VP of Marketing Tor Myhren apologized, saying "We missed the mark with this video," adding blather about "creativity." The ad has been pulled from television but not deleted from other Apple platforms

After *White Teeth* novelist Zadie Smith penned an out-of-touch piece in *The New Yorker* about the student protests against the war in Gaza, many began sharing an online interview with *High Life* director Claire Denis in which Denis makes clear her thoughts about Smith's talent as a screenwriter

Mohammad Rasoulof's new film *The Seed of the Sacred Fig* will premiere in competition at Cannes. The director, however, will not be there, as he has been sentenced to flogging, then eight years in prison, on the usual nebulous charges the Iranian government issues to silence filmmakers

Ryan Smith and Allen Cheney, producers of the unreleased movie *Rust*, will host a yacht party at Cannes. Back in the USA, *Rust*'s lead actor and coproducer Alec Baldwin prepares to go on trial for manslaughter in the deadly shooting of the film's cinematographer, Halyna Hutchins

Billionaire financier Warren Buffett, the ninth-richest person in the world, has seen an AI deepfake of himself and compared it to a nuclear weapon. Still, he says AI "has enormous potential for good" and "scamming has always been part of the American scene"

The Art Directors Guild will shutter its Production Design Initiative program, citing high unemployment in movie and TV art-department positions. "We cannot in good conscience encourage" young people to pursue the profession "at this time," the guild said in an email to applicants

The Fall Guy, based on the 1980s TV show, made $65.4 million in its opening weekend playing to many packed houses. Hollywood considers it a flop. One reason posited for its unacceptable level of success: the film is a "mostly non-IP movie," a meaningless category that doesn't exist

1970 Beatles doc *Let It Be* makes long-awaited return in *Lord of the Rings* director Peter Jackson's restoration, only available to Disney+ subscribers; there will be no theatrical or Blu-ray release

Disney reports as a win "nearly" making a profit with their streaming service this quarter. A spokesman responded to questions about recent losses by saying that we will "see prices starting to go up over time in the streaming service mostly because the content we have is worth paying for"

WBD missed earnings estimates again. WBD CEO David Zaslav blames losses on making a Suicide Squad video game. He plans to raise the price of Max subscriptions and lay off more staff. Zaslav went on record as saying that CEO compensation should be tied to stock performance, implying that his is, though it decidedly is not

WBD has announced it will make another *Lord of the Rings* movie, with Peter Jackson supervising

Disney+ and Hulu have announced a cable TV–style bundled streaming package with WBD and Max that greatly favors Disney

Green Book director Peter Farrelly will direct *I Play Rocky*, a biopic covering Sylvester Stallone's early years

Steve Albini is dead but Brian Eno lives on; the ambient music composer / Coldplay producer / oblique strategist has a doc about himself touring the US that uses computer software so that it is "different each time you watch it." The film is called *Eno*. Guess how many times I've watched it?

Mumblecore auteur Joe Swanberg is running an intermittent traveling VHS rental shop, sometimes from the back of a pizza place, that the city of Chicago is trying to find and shut down

A 27-year-old man was shot to death in the lobby of a Regal cinema in Massillon, Ohio

May 19, 2024

The MTV Movie & TV Awards have been canceled for 2024. Speculation as to why includes fear of New York protests against Israel's war in Gaza, and the larger fear people no longer know that MTV still exists

Director–jury president Greta Gerwig was officially serenaded at Cannes with David Bowie's "Modern Love" because of that scene in *Frances Ha* she and Noah Baumbach stole from Leos Carax's *Mauvais Sang*

Annette puppet Baby Annette appeared with Carax at the Cannes screening of his new 41-minute film, *It's Not Me*

The Penske press is desperate for Francis Ford Coppola's *Megalopolis* to fail, and so is *The Guardian*, which published a nonexposé claiming the production of the film was chaotic and weird, Coppola brooded a lot and pondered decisions, he smoked pot and bought a motel, declined to use CGI at times, and got annoyed by *Padre Pio* actor Shia LaBeouf's asking him so many questions

Iranian director Mohammad Rasoulof has escaped Iran, fleeing to Europe after being sentenced to flogging and prison. His film *The Seed of the Sacred Fig* premieres at Cannes. "From today, I am a resident of cultural Iran. I choose exile," he announced

Free streaming service Tubi is starting something called Stubios, which will ask viewers to green-light movies and TV shows. Actor–content creator Issa Rae will oversee the program. If a project does well, Stubios will fund another by the same "Stubiorunner." Fans will be treated like "mini-producers," a Tubi spokesperson said, insisting that this is not Tubi doing user-generated content. First up is a docuseries by and about Lady London, a rapper-songwriter

Thor: Love and Thunder actor Chris Hemsworth announced his feelings were hurt when Martin Scorsese criticized Marvel movies

It's been revealed that somehow the 2022 Marvel movie *Doctor Strange in the Multiverse of Madness* is the fourth-most expensive film ever made, coming in at $414.9 million

Hot Fuzz director Edgar Wright may direct a remake of *Barbarella* and a remake of *The Running Man*

AMC became a meme stock again, then "retreated"

Agent Cody Banks actor Angie Harmon's dog was shot to death by an Instacart delivery man who was using his father's name and the photo of "an older woman" on his Instacart profile

Steve Buscemi was randomly punched in the face on Third Avenue in Manhattan, the latest victim of violence against character actors in the city

May 26, 2024

In order to finance the third part of his epic western tetralogy *Horizon: An American Saga*, actor-director Kevin Costner says he has "knocked on every boat at Cannes"

OpenAI will not use a voice that sounds like *Her* star Scarlett Johansson for its AI voice assistant. Or, more precisely, the company is "working to pause" its phony Johansson voice because Johansson is suing

British directors and men of principle Ken Loach and Mike Leigh have resigned as patrons of the Phoenix Cinema in London because the venue is hosting an Israeli state-sponsored film festival. The fest is called Seret, and its cofounder says that "politics should be kept separate from culture"

Dan Snyder, billionaire Republican investor and former owner of the Washington Commanders, put money into *Border* director Ali Abbasi's Young Trump biopic *The Apprentice* because he thought it would be a flattering portrayal of Trump

Trump's company says it will sue *The Apprentice* for its "blatantly false accusations," and for being "garbage" and "pure fiction." They've sent a cease-and-desist letter and compared the film to "the illegal Biden Trials," fancifully adding that the movie "doesn't even deserve a place in the straight-to-DVD section of a bargain bin at a soon-to-be-closed discount movie store, it belongs in a dumpster fire"

Steven Rales, honcho of Santa Monica, Calif.'s Indian Paintbrush Productions and producer of Wes Anderson films, has purchased the Criterion Collection and Janus Films lock, stock, and closet

A private investment firm called Naussany Investments & Private Lending tried to skunk *Zola* actor Riley Keough out of Graceland by selling the property at auction in a scam. Keough is Elvis's granddaughter and heir. The company claimed her mother owed them money

Pixar is laying off 14% of its staff as part of Disney CEO Bob Iger's plan to emphasize "quality over quantity." According to NBC News, one of Disney's problems is that "many audience members started to feel [Pixar's] content had grown overly existential and too concerned with social issues beyond the reach of children"

Iger has also mentioned that filmmakers in Hollywood have to "embrace the change" represented by AI

In explaining the all-white cast of his movie *Star Wars*, George Lucas mentioned that robots are discriminated against in his films, just like people discriminate against AI now

Google and Facebook, I mean Alphabet and Meta, are trying to get Hollywood studios to license their libraries for AI training, offering large cash packages

American Pie actor Natasha Lyonne has invested in an AI studio called Late Night Labs

Thor: Ragnarok actor Cate Blanchett announced at Cannes that she is middle class, "with a bit of a white savior complex"

Even though he did the Buzzfeed Puppy Interview, film director John Krasinski's new children's movie *IF* has not done well at the box office

Netflix has released a "universe" called Nextworld in the gaming platform Roblox. *Is It Cake?* will finally be available in interactive 3D

Nobody likes *Atlas*, the $100 million action movie Netflix has made starring *Enough* actor Jennifer Lopez. It's the latest in a series of poorly reviewed would-be blockbusters released by the streamer, which continues to try to bust blocks where there ain't no blocks to bust

Former Netflix Chief Marketing Officer Bozoma Saint John will join the cast of *The Real Housewives of Beverly Hills*

Continuing mismanagement at Toronto's Hot Docs documentary film festival has now led to the closing of the fest's movie theater and the layoff of more staff

A judge has denied *Rust* actor Alec Baldwin's request for a dismissal of his manslaughter charge and the trial will proceed

WBD CEO David Zaslav, at the behest of 81-year-old racist billionaire Disney investor Nelson Peltz, has quashed the documentary *Peltz Beckhams vs the Wedding Planners*, about *Lola* director Nicola Peltz Beckham's lawsuit against her and soccer–Spice Girl scion Brooklyn Beckham's wedding planners. Nicola is Nelson's daughter

Triangle of Sadness director Ruben Östlund has purchased a 747 airliner to make his next film, *The Entertainment System Is Down*, with Kirsten Dunst starring. It's subject, says the Swedish director, is "what happens when we take away entertainment"

"The dogs were good again this year" at Cannes, proclaims *The New York Times*

June 2, 2024

This week's surprise guest star: the Commonwealth of Massachusetts

A device that looked like ordnance that *Captain America: Civil War* actor Chris Evans signed in 2016 at a USO appearance was not a bomb, he now claims, but "an inert object used for training or display purposes only"

The term "naughty popcorn bucket" has now entered the English language, courtesy of Marvel Studios President Kevin Feige, who has OK'd one for sale (not cheap) at screenings of the forthcoming *Deadpool & Wolverine*. Feige's is a parody of the gross *Dune: Part Two* popcorn container

Otis College in Los Angeles commissioned a report that finds Hollywood labor is in decline as the industry becomes dominated by middle managers, computer programmers, and miscellaneous people posing as creatives

Articles in *Business Insider* and *The Los Angeles Times* purporting to be about poor box office performance over Memorial Day weekend finally admitted that the problem with theatrical exhibition is that it costs too much money to go to the movies, regardless of what's playing

The archive of *Golden Boat* actor–performance artist–genius Vito Acconci has fallen into the hands of notorious Brooklyn landlords/gentrifiers Two Trees Management, who claim it is theirs because Acconci, who died in 2017, owed them back rent

Nuts actor Richard Dreyfuss, booked to appear at the Cabot movie theater in Beverly, Mass., where he would introduce a screening of *Jaws*, entered, stage right, wearing a house dress over his clothes while performing a mock-sexy dance. Instead of discussing the Steven Spielberg–directed blockbuster in which he costars, Dreyfuss ranted about trans issues and Barbra Streisand's ability as a film director

Reacting to criticism from *Dirty Grandpa* actor Robert De Niro, convicted felon Donald Trump ended a long social media rant with "Where have you gone Joe Dimaggio!!!," which is normally written as a question and comes from the Simon & Garfunkel song "Mrs. Robinson" in *The Graduate*

Vanity Fair France photoshopped out a Palestinian-flag pin that *Domino* actor Guy Pearce was wearing on his tuxedo in an official portrait taken at Cannes

The newest trend on the red carpet at Cannes this year was having a blonde French security guard harass Black, Dominican, Ukrainian, and Korean women

Immaculate director Michael Mohan has apologized for how dark his horror film looks now that it has debuted on streaming services, blaming the inadequate digital compression standards of the various platforms

Blumhouse Productions will reboot *The Exorcist* with a "radical new take" on the film's "universe." Will a little girl possess the body of the devil this time?

A 245-minute video essay by YouTuber Jenny Nicholson examines the failure in 2023 of Disney's pricey Star Wars: Galactic Starcruiser hotel after one year of operation. The video has gone viral and is described as an "exhaustive" takedown of the shuttered Disney hostelry/miscalculation

A selling point of the forthcoming TV series *Star Wars: The Acolyte* is that it "requires zero *Star Wars* homework"

Lucasfilm president Kathleen Kennedy has admitted that *Star Wars* actresses struggle with harassment from the franchise's fan base of male sociopaths

The New York Times has published a shocking piece of propaganda—for Netflix. Writer Lulu Garcia-Navarro's interview with CEO Ted Sarandos begins with her admission that she and her husband are Netflix addicts, before getting Sarandos on record as saying that streaming makes the world a safer place, that if an audience likes something it means by Netflix's metric it is "quality," and that *Barbie* and *Oppenheimer* would have been just as big if they were Netflix movies, but that *big*, as in screen size, is relative and doesn't matter. Sarandos ends by coming out in favor of AI, explaining that AI will not take people's jobs in general, but the person who is good at AI will take your job in particular

An additional piece in the *Times* by a TV critic claims that motion capture of actors is now so convincing and so moving that it will save cinema, citing Gollum in the *Lord of the Rings* movies and *Kingdom of the Planet of the Apes* as his examples

The viral, AI-generated "All Eyes on Rafah" image—the one that looks like something from Pixar's 2013 Chipotle ad campaign and is being shared on social media to promote awareness of the war in Gaza—is being lauded by some for being better than a real image because of its anodyne quality and fakeness. Their claim is that because the image does not contain graphic content it is more shareable, and will therefore succeed in bringing greater awareness to the pro-Palestinian cause

A new streaming service called either Showrunner or Fable will allow users to create their own shows using AI

Sony Pictures has announced that it will use AI to cut production costs

New York City's Tribeca Festival, which, to enhance its status as America's most generic and boring fest, no longer uses "film" in its name, will show AI-generated shorts made using OpenAI's Sora

Four girls, ages 9–17, were stabbed at a Braintree, Mass., AMC theater during a screening of film director John Krasinski's *IF* by a 26-year-old named Jared Ravizza, who fled the theater in a Porsche, then stabbed two more people at a nearby McDonald's

Ravizza, who has blond flowing locks and is deeply tanned, purports to be from Chilmark on Martha's Vineyard and claims to be the CEO of a digital-marketing agency called Ravizza Jones, based in "Beverly Hills, Malibu, Manhattan, Greenwich, Palm Beach, Paris, and Milan," as well as a model, professional skier, and "serial entrepreneur," and has filed to change his name to Jared Love Jones

Ravizza, who is actually from Agawam, Mass., and is also a suspect in a recent murder in Deep River, Conn., has been compared to Buffalo Bill in *The Silence of the Lambs*, and was said to have had the affect of Jack Nicholson in *The Shining* as he conducted his rampage. Photos of Ravizza, however, prove the news media has completely forgotten the name Jeff Spicoli and the movie *Fast Times at Ridgemont High*

June 9, 2024

Ishana Night Shyamalan, daughter of *After Earth* director M. Night Shyamalan, has joined the Cronenberg children in their nepo baby horror-movie-directing careers. Her debut feature, *The Watchers*, came out this week to middling reviews

Maestro actor Maya Hawke, daughter of actors Ethan Hawke and Uma Thurman, says she is fine owing her career to nepotism. "There are so many people who deserve to have this kind of life who don't," she explains, "but I think I'm comfortable with not deserving it and doing it anyway"

Black Panther actor Lupita Nyong'o, on the other hand, admitted to some discomfort while promoting her new movie *A Quiet Place: Day One*, stating that press junkets are "torture." *Oppenheimer* actor Cillian Murphy said the same in February, calling the movie-publicity system "a broken model"

The Penske Media publication *Variety* somehow got *Gummo* actor Chloë Sevigny to sit down and talk with reality TV performer Kim Kardashian. Differences between the two women emerged during their conversation, including in matters of film taste

Pearl Harbor actor Alec Baldwin, his wife Hilaria (a yoga instructor from Massachusetts named Hillary Hayward-Thomas who likes to pretend she's Spanish from Spain and once claimed to forget the English word "cucumber" during a cooking segment on the *Today* show), and their seven children (who all have Spanish names) will star in a reality TV show for TLC called *The Baldwins* (not *Los Baldwins*) that will air in 2025

In other Alec Baldwin news, the now-imprisoned *Rust* armorer who handed Baldwin the gun with which he shot cinematographer Halyna Hutchins (without pulling the trigger, he claims) has announced she can't wait to testify against him in his upcoming manslaughter trial

The Hutchins family has initiated an additional lawsuit against Baldwin in their daughter's death

Ghosts of Abu Ghraib documentary director Rory Kennedy, who is the daughter of assassinated politician Robert F. Kennedy, has refused to turn over to prosecutors footage from the *Rust* set she expects will be part of a film she is making about the deadly incident. A judge has backed Kennedy, saying her work is protected under a California law that shields journalists from having to give unpublished material to prosecutors in court cases

The Salem Media Group, which distributes the debunked voter-fraud pseudodocumentary *2000 Mules*, will no longer handle the film, admitting it's a tissue of lies. *2000 Mules* was made by Dinesh D'Souza, the prolific conspiracy theorist and convicted felon who was pardoned by Donald Trump. Evidently Salem will not be returning the millions of dollars *2000 Mules* has made from its audience of dupes

Former Trump aide and former *Breitbart* boss Steve Bannon, the producer of Julie Taymor's *Titus* and several *2000 Mules*-esque pseudodocs, has been ordered to report to jail on July 1, where he must serve his four-month sentence for contempt of Congress during the J6 hearings. Bannon is wailing about going to the Supreme Court to get out of it

In a special presentation that was shot like a morning TV talk show, Paramount Global's non-CEO Shari Redstone reassured shareholders about the company's new CEO trio, emphasizing that they want to reduce costs through job cuts and build up the company's failing streaming platform, Paramount+. Later in the week it became clear that they were instead planning to ditch Paramount+ by merging it with some other yet-to-be-announced company's streaming platform

WBD is raising subscription prices on their streaming service Max by a dollar a month, to $16.99 or $20.99, depending on which plan subscribers choose. But what if it came with Paramount+? Worth it?

A growing movement called #DontStreamOnMax is protesting the WBD streaming service for canceling series they liked

A corporate-responsibility watchdog group called As You Sow has ranked WBD CEO David Zaslav the most overpaid CEO in America because he was handed close to a quarter billion dollars in 2022 and delivered to shareholders a nonreturn of -11.6%

Doctor Sleep director Mike Flanagan, who is rebooting *The Exorcist* radically, has apologized to Netflix for expressing disappointment in the streaming studio for not releasing Blu-rays of its films

Movie theater chain Alamo Drafthouse is in the midst of a union drive in response to mismanagement by its owner, Altamont Capital, a private-equity firm that bought the chain in 2021. Additionally, five Alamo theaters have just shut down, all owned by the same franchisee in the Dallas–Fort Worth area, who mismanaged them into bankruptcy

In the latest stop on the Beatlemania gravy train, *Road to Perdition* director Sam Mendes has announced he has hired four popular, handsome actors (Harris Dickinson, Paul Mescal, Barry Keoghan, and Charlie Rowe) to portray the Beatles in a series of four interlocked biopics

Lionsgate's forthcoming Michael Jackson biopic, *Michael* (not to be confused with the Nora Ephron movie in which John Travolta plays an angel), will be the centerpiece in the studio's switch to an IP focus that will probably also include new *Hunger Games* and *John Wick* movies

When *Despicable Me* composer Pharrell Williams "finally heard the magic words 'you can do it anyway you want,'" he "knew deep down inside" that he "wanted to do it through Lego," he says about his forthcoming self-produced animated auto-biopic/documentary, *Piece by Piece*

The Marubo, a remote, reclusive Indigenous group who live in the Amazon rainforest in Brazil, have been hooked up to Starlink courtesy of an American "space entrepreneur" named Allyson Reneau, who has eleven children and wants to one day walk on Mars

Now many of the younger Marubo are obsessed with social media and internet porn, and are abandoning their traditional ways. Marubo elders have had to restrict internet hours, but Flora Dutra, an activist for Indigenous people in Brazil, says any criticism of Marubo internet usage from outside the group is unacceptable ethnocentrism, as if it's the Marubo anyone is criticizing here

The Miss AI beauty pageant, part of Fanvue's World AI Creator Awards, honors top creators of fake women with $20K worth of prizes, including $5K in cash. These male creators assert their pageant is more inclusive than problematic real beauty pageants, because they let all types of women participate, as long as they don't exist

OpenAI and Google DeepMind workers are warning the public about the dangers of AI in an open letter, citing "the risk levels of different kinds of harm," which sounds like something an AI would say

Spread actor Ashton Kutcher, who is an owner of a venture capital firm that invests in AI, made a rambling speech extolling the virtues of OpenAI's Sora, lauding it because it will create "more content than there are eyeballs on the planet"

"Why would you go out and shoot an establishing shot of a house in a television show when you could just create the establishing shot for $100?" Kutcher mused. "To go out and shoot it would cost you thousands of dollars," he explained, though in many cases, it should be said, establishing shots of houses cost less than $100 to make and are often unnecessary lazy filmmaking, and even more money could be saved if they weren't made at all

Mariana Mazzucato, a professor of economics at University College London and founding director of the UCL Institute for Innovation and Public Purpose, writes in *The Guardian* that ChatGPT and other high-tech AI businesses are "guzzling resources," especially water, "at planet-eating rates" due to the vast amounts of energy consumed by cloud-computing data-center "super clusters." The amount of water and electricity required will eventually cripple residential power grids and "undermine water security"

What Professor Mazzucato—an economist—fails to understand is that the money we save using AI to make establishing shots of houses for TV shows can be pumped into environment-saving infrastructure projects that will solve all our problems

June 16, 2024

Who has been rocking my screamboat?

In the least punk rock move in the history of Hollywood, longtime SoCal irritant and *Babylon* actor Flea gave the double bird to photographers on the red carpet at the premiere of the Disney-Pixar animated movie *Inside Out 2*, in which the Red Hot Chili Peppers bassist voices a cop named Jake. That's right, a cop

Good Time actor Robert Pattinson and *Smile* director Parker Finn are producing a remake of Andrzej Zulawski's *Possession* for Pattinson to star in

A second director has quit the job of helming the *Blade* remake for Marvel Studios

During a recent paid screening, by which I mean a regular show on their schedule, Manhattan's ritzy Paris Theater, which is owned by Netflix, was caught projecting *The Conformist* from an Amazon Prime stream of the movie

Sony Pictures is buying the Alamo Drafthouse theater chain. While the 1948 Paramount Consent Decrees have only been loosely enforced since the 1980s, their elimination during the Trump administration has paved the way for studios to own theaters, which United States v. Paramount Pictures, Inc. had made illegal

The Paramount Global sale to Skydance has fallen through due to greed on the part of Paramount non-CEO Shari Redstone

The free streaming service Tubi continues to pummel Disney+, Netflix, Max, and all other streaming platforms except YouTube in the Nielsen ratings

In its latest assault on meaning, Netflix is selling packaged popcorn called Cult Classic Cheddar Kettle in supermarkets

Apple has released a corporate video explaining that adding ChatGPT to its phones will decrease human interaction and eliminate the need for imagination when telling children bedtime stories

Tribeca [Film] Festival has partnered with OpenAI Sora to hoodwink up-and-coming filmmakers into making AI shorts, which led to a defensive social media meltdown from one of the selected participants, *Nanny* director Nikyatu Jusu, who had previously decried the way Silicon Valley uses BIPOC artists as human shields when it has new spirit-breaking software to peddle

The Academy Museum of Motion Pictures in Los Angeles has revised an exhibit called *Hollywoodland: Jewish Founders and the Making of a Movie Capital* after receiving an open letter from industry professionals accusing the curators of antisemitism for pointing out that the moguls of the studio era were, in the museum's words, predators, tyrants, oppressors, and womanizers

James Cameron on acting, from a recent interview: "Kate [Winslet] and Sigourney Weaver, as well—these are strong-willed people that have mastery over their complete instrument, their mind, their voice, their body, everything. And what makes them a good actor also made them good at learning how to free dive"

Mr. Nanny actor Hulk Hogan, the litigious former wrestler, has introduced a new alcoholic beverage called Real American Beer that is designed "to bring America back together" by exploiting the Dylan Mulvaney–rejecting, antitransgender boycott of Bud Light

Since Disney's *Steamboat Willie* copyright expired, two non-Disney horror movies have been made featuring the original version of Mickey Mouse. The latest is *Screamboat*

Saturday Night Live actor Bowen Yang is fretting about whether he can continue to be honest about movies on his podcast after *Mean Girls* screenwriter Tina Fey appeared on it and mentioned to him that giving his real opinion is bad for his career. She gave as an example: What if you got a script from Emerald Fennell?

At the Vatican, Pope Francis met with 105 comedians from around the world to tell them being funny is important to God, to the human soul, and to oppositional politics. The American contingent included Jimmy Fallon, Chris Rock, Tig Notaro, and Whoopi Goldberg, who in *Sister Act* "got into the habit" by playing a singer forced to hide in a convent and impersonate a nun

June 23, 2024

Sorry to Bother You actor Armie Hammer says he is grateful he was called a cannibal in 2021 and that he is now on a hero's journey, which means he's working on a screenplay

The next Percival Everett book to get a big-screen adaptation will be his most recent novel, *James*. In what can only be described as a worst-case scenario, the film will be produced by Steven Spielberg and directed by Taika Waititi

Netflix is opening two businesses that they are calling Netflix House, one in Dallas, Tex., the other in King of Prussia, Pa. These buildings, which look like cineplex movie theaters, will feature attractions based on Netflix TV series *Bridgerton*, *Squid Game*, *Stranger Things*, and, one hopes, *Fuller House*

Five men were convicted in Las Vegas for running an extensive and illegal streaming service called Jetflicks that they had been operating since 2007, and which had netted them "millions of dollars" from their "tens of thousands of subscribers" who were watching "hundreds of thousands" of television series and movies. Do I know anyone who was subscribing to this? If so, you've been awfully quiet about it

The Edinburgh Fringe Festival is having trouble finding people to portray J. K. Rowling and Emma Watson in a play called *Terf* because actresses are afraid appearing in it will hurt their chances of getting roles in HBO's upcoming *Harry Potter* TV series

The Prince Charles Cinema in London is under fire. The movie theater has been forced by public outcry to cancel the screening of a movie called *The Last Screenwriter*, a Swiss movie by Peter Luisi written entirely using ChatGPT

Across the pond, Le Clef cinema in Paris, a storied rep theater housed in a building owned by the Caisse d'Epargne banking group, has been saved by film activists called Cinéma Revival, who have now raised the entire €2 million needed to buy the building after receiving a large cash donation from *Death Proof* director Quentin Tarantino

US Surgeon General Vivek Murthy has called for warning labels to be put on social media sites because they are addictive and cause anxiety and depression. No word from Murthy on whether Letterboxd would be included

Pope Francis remains in movie news this week, announcing that he has a favorite film and it's Fellini's *La Strada*. He better think of three more in case Letterboxd corners him at the Vatican

Amazon/MGM says it is not to blame for three recent accidents on its film sets, two of them on forthcoming Eddie Murphy movies *Candy Cane Lan*e and *The Pickup*, the other on *The Lord of the Rings: The Rings of Power*, whose title alone is an OSHA hazard

Full Metal Jacket actor Matthew Modine has demanded that Amazon Prime restore the phrase "Born to Kill" to the army helmet on the poster for Stanley Kubrick's *Full Metal Jacket*. Amazon has acquiesced, claiming they had a rule disallowing nontitle text on movie thumbnails, which forced them to digitally remove the phrase

Amazon/MGM is developing a sequel to Mel Brooks's 1987 spoof *Spaceballs*, starring unfunny *Frozen* actor Josh Gad

WBD has hired Robert Gibbs, former Obama-administration press secretary, to be their head of communications. Gibbs is good with journalists and will fit right in at Warners. In 2012 he explained that a 16-year-old American citizen killed accidentally by the US in a drone strike in Yemen "should [have] had a more responsible father"

A new documentary called *I Am: Celine Dion* highlights the *Titanic* singer's struggle with stiff-person syndrome and includes a seizure she had while filming. *USA Today*'s Melissa Ruggieri describes the doc this way: "In *I Am: Celine Dion*,

[Dion is] standing onstage, the mania surrounding her every performance in full effect as she plows through Ike and Tina Turner's 'River Deep — Mountain High' in a voice like a tsunami. In the next scene, she's in a fetal position being strapped to a gurney by medics"

Battleship actor Rihanna is voicing Smurfette in the forthcoming *Smurfs* movie, and she has recently recorded some original songs for the animated feature, her first new music since 2016, not counting the song she phoned in for *Black Panther: Wakanda Forever* two years ago

After a five-year absence, *Honey* actor and eco-friendly beauty-products CEO Jessica Alba has returned to the screen to star in a Netflix action movie called *Trigger Warning*, which premiered this week to bad reviews

Reindeer Games actor Ben Affleck has purchased a new Airstream RV and had it delivered to his home in Brentwood. The *Air* director will now be able to flee Hollywood like Joel McCrea in *Sullivan's Travels*, but not like Albert Brooks in *Lost in America*, because he won't have a wife with him. In any case, we should remind him to be careful with his nest egg

Harder They Fall actor Jonathan Majors, through with the domestic violence–intervention program that resulted from his conviction for assault, will star in a "supernatural revenge thriller" called *Merciless*, to be directed by Denis Villeneuve's little brother, Martin

Add *Mothman Prophecies* actor Debra Messing to the list of women Donald Trump has a weird, wounded crush on. He claims she said she was grateful *The Apprentice* boosted ratings for her TV series *Will & Grace*, he thinks she's "quite attractive," but she's also a Democrat and she has mentioned on social media that he's a crap dog, or words to that effect. He can't get his mind around it

Kevin Costner is defending casting his 15-year-old son in a prominent role in his forthcoming *Horizon: An American Saga* movies because "he is a beautiful boy"

On the cover of his new book *Dear Orson Welles (and Other Essays)*, film critic Mark Cousins is sprawled across seven seats in a movie theater, dressed in a black T-shirt and black shorts, his eyes closed and his head thrown back, presumably because he is experiencing the ecstasy of moviegoing and not merely asleep. As a fellow film critic, one thing I've noticed in my work is that it's hard to see the movie with your eyes closed

June 30, 2024

Chinatown screenwriter Robert Towne, age 89, and *Mank* director David Fincher will be doing a *Chinatown*–prequel series for Netflix

Have you ever wondered what would happen if a 37-year-old woman swapped bodies with a 65-year-old woman? Disney's forthcoming sequel, *Freakier Friday*, with Lindsay Lohan and Jamie Lee Curtis returning from the original remake, will presumably answer that question

Beowulf director Robert Zemeckis's next film is called *Here*. It is shot from a fixed point of view in a living room and features de-aged and up-aged Tom Hanks and Robin Wright seen through many years, although evidently the film is somehow more about the living room

Hallmark is teaming up with the Kansas City Chiefs football team to make a Christmas movie called *Holiday Touchdown: A Chiefs Love Story*

Horror director Ti West seems to have staged a fake protest outside a theater in Hollywood to promote his new film, *Maxxxine*

The Revue Cinema in Toronto is on the brink of closing because their landlord wants to raise the rent so much. Meanwhile, the West Newton Cinema outside Boston appears to have raised enough money to purchase itself and remain in operation

Many screenwriters and actors in Hollywood are on the brink of losing their health insurance because the strikes last year limited the amount they could work, meaning they will not meet the union work-time minimums that allow them to maintain their plans

There was a long article in *The New York Times* in which the major villains of the streaming era, including Ted Sarandos and John Malone, gathered on Barry Diller's yacht to discuss "the future of streaming," which was the title of the piece

WBD's Max is bringing back the HBO brand because no one likes Max

Sony, Universal, and WBD are suing various AI start-ups for using their copyrighted material to train content-generating AI systems

Microsoft AI CEO Mustafa Suleyman says it's OK to do that because "the social contract" of the web implies that all online content is "freeware" and therefore can be used for training AI

Movie studio A24 has secured a large investment from Thrive Capital, a finance firm specializing in AI run by Josh Kushner, Jared Kushner's brother. Thrive is a major investor in OpenAI and is helping pitch their Sora product to studios

The first-ever all-AI TV commercial has been created, and it's for Toys"R"Us, which I thought had gone out of business. Toys seem like an odd use for that, since they already exist and kids like to see them in action. Maybe they're not real toys?

Headline of the Week: "Faces made of living skin make robots smile"

Paramount+ is raising its subscription prices while also cutting all the content on its Comedy Central, TV Land, MTV, and Country Music Television websites

The South by Southwest festival, aka SXSW, aka "South by," a Penske Media property, has dropped its partnerships with various arms manufacturers and the US military after being boycotted because of its complicity with the Israeli apartheid regime's genocidal war in Gaza

The new Netflix rom-com *A Family Affair*, featuring an all-star cast led by Nicole Kidman and Zac Efron, has premiered to terrible reviews and low audience scores, and is the first film I have ever seen a Penske Media property describe as "puzzlingly uncinematic"

Relatedly, *The New York Times* thinks Catherine Breillat's new film, *Last Summer*, about a woman sleeping with her stepson, "may shock" its viewers

The perpetrator of the Graceland scam meant to rob *Mad Max: Fury Road* actor Riley Keough of her birthright as Elvis's granddaughter appears to have been an elderly conwoman in Missouri posing as a Nigerian

Streets of Fire actor Willem Dafoe played *Nosferatu* actor Max Schreck in the 2000 film *Shadow of the Vampire*, which was a fictionalized account of the making of *Nosferatu*. Now Dafoe will play the Van Helsing character in a remake of *Nosferatu* in which *It* actor Bill Skarsgård will play the Nosferatu role

The dog of *Lola* director Nicola Peltz Beckham has died at a dog groomer operating out of a van, and the heiress-auteur is going to sue after she finishes a series of social media posts about her "unbearable pain"

Billionaire Brinah Milstein and her husband Roy Bank, a producer of reality TV shows including *It's Worth What?*, own the house Marilyn Monroe died in. They want to tear it down after having purchased it a year ago for $8.35 million. The couple lives in the residence next door and wants to expand. The Los Angeles City Council has stopped them by declaring the Monroe house a landmark

Marry Me actor Jennifer Lopez was spotted flying coach, and we were told that humanizes her

A new phenomenon has been identified among men flying on airplanes who don't watch movies, listen to music, read books, or look at their devices during long flights, opting instead to just stare at the on-screen flight tracker, and think. It has been named "rawdogging," and as soon as an article appeared about it, it was denounced as essentialist and said on social media not to be an actual thing. Reader, I have done this. Does that humanize me?

July 6, 2024

Asked in an interview by the Penske Media publication *The Hollywood Reporter* to comment on the current state of the film industry, *Unsane* director Steven Soderbergh said, "Everybody is terrified about everything"

The Tim Burton *Beetlejuice* sequel, *Beetlejuice Beetlejuice*, will open the Venice Film Festival at the end of August. Is this the first time an IP sequel has opened a major international film festival? I think it is

The film of the Broadway musical *Wicked* and the sequel *Gladiator II* will be coming out the same day in late November, and entertainment journalists are asserting that this is another Barbenheimer situation

Portrait of a Lady on Fire actor Noémie Merlant is starring in a remake of the 1970s softcore hit *Emmanuelle* that will come out in September

The greed of Paramount Global's non-CEO Shari Redstone has now been satisfied, and the sale of her studio to Skydance will go through

The ShowPlace Icon movie theater in Chicago has gone out of business, taking the small chain it was part of with it

Redbox has gone bankrupt. Soon you will no longer be able to rent DVDs and Blu-rays from machines in front of supermarkets and 7–Elevens. The company was owned by Chicken Soup for the Soul Entertainment. Did they own Redbox because actual non-metaphorical cans of chicken soup are sold at the same places Redbox machines are parked?

Most of Netflix's and Amazon's new productions for streaming are now foreign TV series, in a trend set to continue, which will diminish US television and film production

A company called ElevenLabs has licensed the AI-generated voices of Judy Garland, James Dean, Burt Reynolds, and Laurence Olivier to record audiobooks "and other text material"

A Democratic operative writing in *HuffPost* has suggested that the voice of the still-living Joe Biden be enhanced using AI, along with other aspects of his being, to improve his performance on TV and radio, which will allow voters to "focus on his substance"

The Japanese telecom conglomerate Softbank plans to use AI to modulate the voices of angry customers so that their call center service representatives don't get stressed

Other companies with call centers have begun using AI to make their customer-service reps outside the US sound as if they are speaking in "non-accented American English"

Google set goals to mitigate the effects of climate change at their company, but they have now announced they have no chance of meeting them because of the amount of electricity needed to run their AI projects

If you saw the "pretty stunning AI spaghetti art" video clip and its attendant responses from AI industry personnel this week, you know that the mentalities of these people have been deteriorating even faster than expected

Netflix is trying to make a big deal about how the well-known theme music in their *Beverly Hills Cop* sequel, *Beverly Hills Cop: Axel F*, was produced using "the original synths"

Kanye West's porn production company has produced nothing and may not exist, yet it has employees who are being abused, referred to as slaves, and are subject to other unfair labor practices. They are suing

Titus producer and former Trump advisor Steve Bannon is now in federal prison, where he is to spend four months behind bars

Mystic River actor Kevin Bacon dressed as "a regular person" in a prosthetic mask and went to the Grove in LA, where he went unrecognized and had to wait in line for coffee. "I was like, this sucks," he said about the experience, which was seemingly more promotion for horror director Ti West's *Maxxxine*, in which Bacon appears

The *A Quiet Place* sequel, *A Quiet Place: Day One*, ends with the protagonist (Lupita Nyong'o) listening to Nina Simone's song "Feeling Good," the very same song the protagonist (Kōji Yakusho) of last year's Wim Wenders's movie *Perfect Days* listens to at the end of that movie—yet somehow reviews of *A Quiet Place: Day One* don't mention this

In an interview in the Penske Media publication *Variety*, *Palo Alto* actor and Belletrist book club cofounder Emma Roberts discussed film criticism. "Where it used to be like five people reviewed a movie, and now it's like you have people that won't even say what their real name is saying how much they hate something," she explained, then went on to suggest that the solution would be for people to include their driver's license numbers on their Instagram accounts so that they would think twice before saying "something rude"

July 14, 2024

We will all remember where we were when we found out former president Donald Trump's right ear was grazed by a bullet and/or by shattered teleprompter glass. I, for instance, was watching a nine-month-old For Your Consideration Blu-ray screener of Sofia Coppola's *Priscilla*

Batman & Robin actor George Clooney has called for Joe Biden to give up his campaign to be reelected president

WBD honcho David Zaslav was at an investment bank's media conference in Idaho this week, where he called for the next American president—he does not care who—to completely deregulate the film and television industries, so that "we can do what we need to do to be even better"

Another argument against the consolidation of wealth is the ultralavish Ambani wedding in India, a monthslong celebration paid for by the [other] ninth-richest man in the world, to which he has invited Bollywood and Hollywood stars and international politicians too numerous to mention, one of which was former UK prime minister Boris Johnson, a dream wedding guest if there ever was one

What proves all this is so wrong? Spending $10 million to have Justin Bieber sing for the lucky couple. If you could afford to have any musician or musicians perform at your wedding, where would Justin Bieber be on your list? Not first

Pearl Harbor actor Alec Baldwin's trial for manslaughter in New Mexico began with his non-Spanish wife Hilaria holding up their baby for photographers and ended in a mistrial as the judge dismissed the charges against Baldwin "with prejudice"

because prosecutors had withheld evidence. Baldwin is now free to act again, and his forthcoming reality show with Hilaria and their seven kids just got a lot less interesting

Flawless, an "AI-driven filmmaking studio," is proposing that their software TrueSync be used to dub actors' voices in foreign films by digitally mapping new lip movements onto actors' faces. The company has already acquired some foreign titles to mar this way, claiming that this VFX work will comply with union labor laws

Disney has allegedly become the victim of a 1.1 TB data hack that has stolen a massive amount of information on unreleased projects. So far only gamer and comic book websites are reporting this, saying a hacker or hacking group with the excellent name NullBulge is responsible

After last month's box office failure of *Postman* director Kevin Costner's *Horizon: An American Saga—Chapter 1*, *Horizon: An American Saga—Chapter 2* will not be released in theaters next month as originally planned

The troubled production of WBD's *Captain America: Brave New World* continued apace as it was revealed that an Israeli superhero's backstory has been retconned, turning her from a former Mossad agent into a former Black Widow. The actor who plays her, Shira Haas, is herself a former volunteer in the IDF who was medically exempt from service

Apocalypto director Mel Gibson has written a letter of support to excommunicated archbishop Carlo Maria Viganò expressing his support for the defrocked archconservative priest. Throughout the missive Gibson refers to the current pontiff as

Jorge Bergoglio instead of as Pope Francis, because he, the director of *The Passion of the Christ*, does not accept the "false, post conciliar church" as legit

The British cineplex chain Cineworld will close 25 of its 100 theaters. Among the cinemas the corporation will shutter is London's 94-year-old showplace the Fulham Road Picture House. On Twitter, *Cloud Atlas* actor Hugh Grant reacted to the closure by writing "Let's all sit at home and watch << content >> on << streaming >>. While scrolling. Miserable face emoji"

Fury Road actor Zoë Kravitz has been forced to change the name of her feature-film directorial debut from *Pussy Island* to *Blink Twice*. Kravitz says she understands the original title tested poorly with women and that we as a society "are not ready to embrace p - - - y yet"

An extra on the set of *Maxxxine* is suing star Mia Goth for kicking him in the head and then taunting him when he went to use the bathroom, telling him "Nobody will believe you because you're nothing." The lawsuit is real but it's impossible to tell if the incident really happened after director Ti West's winky guerrilla marketing for the film

Scottish film critic and TV presenter Mark Cousins took the occasion of the great Shelley Duvall's death to tweet that Robert Altman only made ten good movies. When the tattooed essayist was challenged, he insulted his readers by calling their defenses of Altman "knowledge-free opinions"

Disney has plans to make a *Devil Wears Prada* sequel with the original cast returning. The film will update fashion-magazine publishing to the digital age, which I guess will entail laying off everyone except Meryl Streep, who will get a raise, and Anne Hathaway will move to Columbia County to write a parenting book

There will be a *Shrek 5*, with the original voice cast returning

Tiny Furniture director Lena Dunham has pulled out of directing *Polly Pocket*, which is supposed to be the next Mattel x WBD collab after *Barbie*. Instead, Dunham will pivot to making two TV series for Netflix. She cites artistic restraints and body-shaming issues as reasons for her exit

Coneheads actor Ellen DeGeneres has announced she will retire from show business after her forthcoming Netflix comedy special airs, a reaction to her being outed as a meanie

Fans are theorizing that the reason season 3 of the Netflix TV series *Bridgerton* was so bad was because it was at least partially written by AI

Bob's Burgers actor Jay Johnston has pleaded guilty to attacking the US Capitol on January 6, 2021, and now faces five years in prison

Sex and the City actor John Corbett says he regrets becoming an actor and now feels he chose "the wrong thing to do" with his life

This week *Oppenheimer* actor Jack Quaid, the son of Dennis Quaid and Meg Ryan, continued the new trend in nepo baby attitudinizing by admitting his advantage in Hollywood while soft-pedaling it at the same time. Meg Ryan, he says, is just being a good mom by defending him from detractors as she paves the way for his success

The decimation of Generation X continued this week with the death of *Heathers* actor Shannen Doherty, age 53

Emerald Fennell's *Wuthering Heights*

July 21, 2024

Hours before President Joe Biden dropped out of the race to be reelected, *The New York Times* published a bizarre op-ed by *Trial of the Chicago 7* writer-director Aaron Sorkin calling for the Democratic Party to nominate Republican senator Mitt Romney as its candidate for president

In other Utah news, now that Park City has decided not to renew the Sundance Film Festival's agreement with the town to host the fest, Sundance has announced five potential new host cities nobody from Hollywood wants to go to: Atlanta, Boulder, Cincinnati, Louisville, and Santa Fe

The Disney leak of 1.1 TB of data on unreleased projects by the hacktivist or hacktivists called NullBulge was prompted by Disney's disregard for artists' rights, its approach to AI, and its exploitation of consumers, according to the outlaw group. Apparently NullBulge infiltrated Disney's servers as early as May

Disney is removing its animatronic character Liver Lips McGrowl from their theme parks' Country Bear Jamboree. The company went out of its way in a press release to explain that LLMcG was offensive to alcoholics because of his appearance, and that "liver lips" is a pejorative term for people with cirrhosis—and, also, incidentally, by the way, the look of the character could be considered offensive to Black people

WBD CEO David Zaslav has a plan to raise the company's stock price by breaking up the company into component parts. Not sure how that would work or do anything at all

WBD's HBO is planning a TV series based on the 2002 Brazilian movie *City of God*. Not sure how that would work or do anything at all

Bulworth actor Halle Berry has dropped out of starring in a forthcoming Ryan Murphy TV series called *All's Fair*, which the media portrayed as an example of her continuing uncanny ability to avoid crap TV work, which would be admirable and true if she hadn't starred in the CBS TV series *Extant* in 2014

Berry also this week blamed the failure of her 2004 movie *Catwoman* on critics

That's part of a renewed trend this week that included *Green Book* actor Viggo Mortensen, who while decrying the Amazon-only release of his 2022 movie *Thirteen Lives* also claimed that "what passes for critical thinking in terms of reviews is pretty poor" these days

And Republican vice-presidential nominee JD Vance, who supposedly went full Trumper because of the terrible reviews the Netflix movie of his book *Hillbilly Elegy* received

Thirteen Lives and *Hillbilly Elegy*, it should be noted, were both directed by Ron Howard

After Kyle Gass, Jack Black's partner in the musical comedy duo Tenacious D, wished, during a Tenacious D performance in Australia, that the bullet had not missed Trump, Black issued a statement saying that the joke "blindsided" him. Black then canceled the Tenacious D tour and broke with Gass professionally. Black stars in the movie franchises *Kung Fu Panda*, *Jumanji*, *Goosebumps*, *Super Mario Bros.*, and *Minecraft*

Silence of the Lambs actor Anthony Hopkins had never heard about Donald Trump's obsession with Hannibal Lecter until last week. In addition to frequently name-checking the fictional serial killer / supergenius Hopkins played, Trump has also asserted that Hopkins is dead and that he supported Trump in 2016, both erroneous claims

At the Republican National Convention, AI screens used as backdrops featured American flags with 70 stars instead of 50, perhaps in celebration of the second Trump administration's potential annexations of all Canada's provinces, Greenland's municipalities, and Bermuda

Studios are starting to microslice success metrics the way broadcast TV began to do as it lost viewership to streaming. Thus, the *Twister* sequel, *Twisters*, leads the box office this week, but also had "the biggest start ever for a natural disaster pic." *Twisters*, incidentally, does not mention climate change despite its subject, because *Minari* director Lee Isaac Chung didn't want to be seen as "putting forward any message"

Disney's Marvel Studios is returning to the more recent past by hiring the Russo brothers to direct the next two *Avengers* movies. The next two?

Season 26 of the CBS reality TV series *Big Brother* will feature something called BB AI, which will somehow run the show, making it "the most unpredictable season for Houseguests," a phrase that already seems AI generated. The disgraced, indefatigable Julie Chen Moonves will return to host alongside what appears to be hologram of herself

The 9,500-square-foot, $27 million San Francisco mansion of OpenAI CEO Sam Altman is falling apart because the eyebrow-less tech whiz hired a shady contractor, whom he is now suing. Part of the problem is that the Lombard Street house's sewage line was plugged up with bags by a pissed-off subcontractor, causing flooding and attracting coyotes to the patio

The founder of NBCUniversal and WBD's crappy movie-ticket-selling app Fandango, J. Michael Cline, has committed suicide by jumping from a high floor of Midtown Manhattan's Kimberly Hotel. The depressed investment banker was also a former employee of McKinsey & Company

Pearl Harbor actor Alec Baldwin, not content to get off scot-free for manslaughter, says he will now sue the State of New Mexico for everything he went through

The new *Alien: Romulus* popcorn bucket has a distinct sex-toy look like the other ones made as in-theater promotions this summer, and if I were an editor I would assign someone a piece on why these things all look like they were made for coitus

July 28, 2024

As soon as Joe Biden dropped out of the race to be reelected president, *Trial of the Chicago 7* writer-director Aaron Sorkin immediately recanted his suggestion, from his *New York Times* op-ed, that the Democratic Party nominate failed Republican candidate Mitt Romney in his stead. In a *Times*-approved rewrite,

Sorkin pivoted to providing the Dems with un-asked-for, generalized "scripting" advice

While the Fox Village Theatre in Westwood will remain open, saved by a consortium of film directors led by *Ghostbusters: Afterlife* director Jason Reitman, its twin theater across the way, the Bruin, a Streamline Moderne landmark that was seen in *Once Upon a Time in Hollywood*, will shutter, probably permanently. Quentin Tarantino can't save every movie theater

For the first times in years, Netflix will have no films in the Venice Film Festival, which starts in one month

The Toronto International Film Festival starts in a little over a month, and for the first time fest curators are making short videos "offering insights" into their choices. For instance, in one made by programmer Jane Schoettle, she explains that the films she selected have the themes of "healing" and "love," and that taken together they are like a box of chocolates. She did not mention *Forrest Gump* by name

Amazon Prime Video (not Amazon MGM Studios) has purchased the Bray Studios outside London, former home of Hammer Film Productions

Northwell Health, which is New York's largest owner of hospitals and outpatient facilities, is opening a film studio to develop scripted film and TV content and reality shows. Northwell Studios will use doctors, nurses, and patients in these productions, and has previously allowed its facilities and personnel to be used as the basis for semidocumentary entertainment by HBO and Netflix. Northwell Health has been sued by the State of New York for deceptive advertising practices and by competitors for trademark infringements, and has been plagued with billing problems

Former Netflix film-production chief Scott Stuber will now run United Artists, the studio founded by Chaplin, Griffith, Pickford, and Fairbanks that was brought low by the release of Michael Cimino's *Heaven's Gate* in 1980, and is now a division of Amazon MGM. Expect lots of rebooted IP on the schedule—I predict new *Pink Panther* movies—and maybe a big auteur project every two years

An exposé in *The Boston Globe* has revealed that the Netflix movie *Don't Look Up* by *Other Guys* director Adam McKay cost Massachusetts taxpayers $46.4 million in tax credits, the largest in commonwealth history, and that Leonardo DiCaprio and Jennifer Lawrence were paid about $60 million between them to appear in the unfunny climate change satire

I don't begrudge McKay his budget or DiCaprio and Lawrence their salaries. This is merely a good opportunity to note two things: the film does not take place in Massachusetts, and it only made $800,000 at the box office before Netflix moved it to streaming, where they claimed that *Don't Look Up* had the highest viewership of any film they had ever released, totaling some 360 million hours, or almost 1 hour for every citizen of the United States

Apple TV+'s little-people-less *Time Bandits* remake TV series, made by Taika Waititi, has been called "wildly offensive," "immediately wrong," and "an ill-advised slog" bereft of "a single amusing concept or witty line" that "strains one's patience to interminable lengths." Actually that was all from one review, Nick Schager's, in *The Daily Beast*. All the other outlets had headlines like "The Gloriously Fun Return of a Fantasy Classic." I wonder who's right?

Early press promised that *Deadpool & Wolverine* "required no Marvel homework" to enjoy. Now every piece about it promises to reveal 18 hidden Easter eggs and lists the 22 Marvel movies you need to see to truly get it

The film's director, Shawn Levy, inadvertently revealed he is redefining "populist" to mean "corporate thralldom," saying he is "not looking to make movies and shows for an audience of seven cool kids in the corner. I build stories for populist entertainment"

Transformers director Michael Bay will make *Skibidi Toilet* films and franchise the internet sensation for TV. His producing partner likens the viral web series to the *John Wick* movies and also brought up *District 9*. The series is made in Russia by a guy named Alexey Gerasimov, who operates under the handle DaFuq!?Boom!

I'd love to know how this Gerasimov is related to the Soviet director Sergei Gerasimov, who made the classic epic *And Quiet Flows the Don* in 1957, as both their work is water based

If there are two bigger pseudoevents than Comic-Con and the Olympics, I'm not sure what they are. So I will only take a cursory look

At the Olympics, the opening ceremony paid tribute to French cinema history, starting with the Lumières' train leaving the station and Méliès's trip to the moon, and ending of course with that French cinema favorite, the Minions

Alice Guy-Blaché, the silent-film pioneer who was perhaps the first person to make a narrative feature film, didn't make the cut and was relegated to a statuary tribute to famous French women

At Comic-Con, a character in a forthcoming *Fantastic Four* reboot was described as "comic-accurate," a term I had not heard before

It was revealed that the White House will be destroyed in *Captain America: Brave New World*. How many more times can the White House be destroyed in Hollywood blockbusters?

David Harbour costars with Florence Pugh in a forthcoming *Thunderbolts* movie. He said of her, not of the movie they are working on, but of her, Florence Pugh, the person, "There's warmth and humor, but there's also a lot of pathos"

Flying in the face of film history more than the French Olympic Committee, Fede Álvarez, the director of *Alien: Romulus*, said that the reason the film's cast is all young people, unlike the first *Alien* movie, is because "the younger the people the tougher it is to watch them die"

This week's critic hater is Tyler Perry. The triple-threat filmmaker told *Nope* actor Keke Palmer in a podcast that he is tired of "highbrows," especially "the highbrow Negro" who drives a Volvo and goes "to therapy on the weekend," stating that to criticize his work is to disenfranchise his audience

Weekend therapy? His imaginary critics must be doing really well

The *Medea* director, as it happens, was not responding to actual critics but to a comedian named Loni Love who suggested he hire more Black writers and directors and not try to do everything himself

Trump is still going on at his rallies about Hannibal Lecter, where he calls the film that made the character infamous *Silence of the Lamb*. The media has offered weird interpretations of this behavior, none of which include the notion that maybe the candidate identifies with serial killers in some deep way

Ryan Reynolds and Hugh Jackman guest hosted Jimmy Kimmel's late-night talk show, where Reynolds made jokes about people fucking the *Deadpool & Wolverine* popcorn bucket

Just as it is hard to imagine FDR ranting about Lon Chaney Jr. as the Wolfman while campaigning, it is impossible to imagine Humphrey Bogart going on TV and talking about fucking a popcorn bucket

A blog post JD Vance penned in 2005 when he was a marine has revealed the Republican vice-presidential candidate to be a man who was very moved by the Zach Braff joint *Garden State*. The post also included a reference to the Gwen Stefani song "Hollaback Girl"

Lemonheads singer-songwriter Evan Dando appears to be back on the dummy pipe and is thread-posting on Twitter about how Javier Bardem in *Skyfall* reminds him of Macaulay Culkin in the *Home Alone* movies

Disgraced producer Harvey Weinstein has COVID (like our president), has been hospitalized, and is in general pulling the sick-and-dying mobster bit as he faces a new trial

The style of idiotic entertainment reporting is starting to infect real news items. Two headlines this week: "Park Fire in Northern California Explodes in Its First Day" and "This Is the Worst Police Shooting Video Ever"

I found out that at my barbershop the most requested haircut is the "Brad Pitt in *Fury*." (I always ask for either the "Michael Chabon" or the "Brett Gurewitz")

August 4, 2024

Lin-Manuel Miranda is making a musical version of Walter Hill's 1979 movie *The Warriors*. Fortunately it is only for a record album. For now

Universal is planning a Britney Spears biopic, based on Spears's 2023 memoir *The Woman in Me*

G.I. Joe: Retaliation director Jon M. Chu will helm the Spears film, following his *Wicked* musical adaptations. An actor to play Britney has not been announced

There will be a *Hunger Games* prequel called *The Hunger Games: Sunrise on the Reaping*. Writer Suzanne Collins says she was inspired by philosopher David Hume in conceiving it

Disney is laying off 2% of its television division, 140 people

Beechwood Cinemas in Athens, Ga., is closing. I learned this from an article in *The Federalist* called "*Twisters*: Summer Blockbuster Succeeds Because It Leaves Sex and Politics Behind," written by the magazine's summer intern, a college student in Athens who attended the Beechwood and was offended by all the sex and politics in the movies they were showing, which at the time of closure includes such controversial fare as *Despicable Me 4* and *Fly Me to the Moon*

The New York Times reports that Hollywood's new message to red states is: "Our movies are for you," explaining that studio movies will now downplay progressive values and "just entertain"

Collateral director Michael Mann is putting his archives online. To view them will cost $65, for which users will get an access code generated by blockchain technology. This of course is for security reasons. We don't want a *Blackhat* situation on our hands

Alt-weeklies, once home to some of the finest film criticism in the land, have become "zombie alt-weeklies," which exist mainly to publish AI-generated stories about OnlyFans models

Continuing the Letterboxd-ification of film criticism, this month's Locarno Film Festival has announced it will give the "Letterboxd Piazza Grande Award" to a new feature film, picked by a jury made up of "Letterboxd editorial staff and young accredited critics." The winning film will receive "extensive editorial coverage on Letterboxd to help build global awareness"

A TV commercial for Google's AI product Gemini features a father using AI to write a fan letter to Olympic sprinter Sydney McLaughlin-Levrone for his daughter, because "this has to be just right." The spot so enraged viewers, and generated so much bad press, that Google first closed comments on the ad's YouTube page and then pulled it entirely

Instagram will allow users to make AI versions of themselves using Meta's AI Studio, moving us one step closer to living in the 2009 Bruce Willis movie *Surrogates*

Both ABC talk show host Jimmy Kimmel and *Chip 'n Dale: Rescue Rangers* voice actor John Mulaney have turned down offers to host the Oscars next year. Unclear if Jo Koy has been asked

Hector David Jr., who has played the green Power Ranger across a variety of *Power Rangers* products, was caught on video in an Idaho parking lot shoving an elderly man to the ground. David was set to appear at the Magic Valley Comic-Con in the town of Twin Falls but instead fled the scene in his car. There is no indication he yelled "Power up!" at the vehicle before speeding away

Robert Downey Jr. and the Russo brothers will be getting even bigger paydays than earlier reported for the next two *Avengers* movies. In addition to the $100 million for Downey and $80 million for the Russos, there will be back-end compensation and "performance escalators" that kick in if the films cross the $750 million and then $1 billion marks at the box office

A Fish Called Wanda actor Jamie Lee Curtis has apologized for insulting Marvel Studios when the Disney division was down and she was riding high with *Everything Everywhere All at Once*. Marvel product is topping the box office again, and Curtis now says her comments "were stupid" and she would do better going forward, with a focus on "communication" instead of "toilet paper promotion"

The *très* wacky Paris Olympics will end with *Tropic Thunder* actor Tom Cruise rappelling down the Stade de France carrying the Olympic torch before cutting to a prefilmed segment in which the *Mission: Impossible* star skydives onto the Hollywood sign, torch in hand. Burn Hollywood burn?

The guy who had a meltdown at the IFC Center in Manhattan and demanded a refund because the theater was not showing the trailer for the forthcoming *Joker* sequel turned out to be a fledgling filmmaker promoting his new project. His short film is about a drug addict obsessed with Lady Gaga and he's trying to raise money for it by going viral. Funny stuff

August 11, 2024

King Richard actor Will Smith for some reason became stranded in Zurich and took a very early morning walk by himself. Alarmed by the lack of other people outside, he made an Instagram video comparing the situation to his movie *I Am Legend*

Country singer Keith Urban gifted a Lamborghini to his wife, *BMX Bandits* actor Nicole Kidman, and somehow it became a news story that Kidman does not drive the car to Target or the supermarket in Nashville, where she and Urban live

Bound actor Jennifer Tilly has joined the cast of the Bravo reality TV series *The Real Housewives of Beverly Hills*, saying for her it's like working with Martin Scorsese. She didn't really explain how it's like that

Good Will Hunting actors Ben Affleck and Matt Damon have announced that they will make a feature film based on the Peter Thiel–Hulk Hogan lawsuit that put *Gawker* out of business. Affleck says he may play Hogan

M. Night Shyamalan's latest film, *Trap*, was labeled "Anti-Brat" in a *Rolling Stone* headline and "most assuredly not brat" in the accompanying review by David Fear, a grown man

While promoting her new movie *Borderlands*, which was made over three years ago and has a 0% rating on Rotten Tomatoes, *Tár* actor Cate Blanchett claimed she was paid in "free sandwiches" to act in *The Lord of the Rings*

Quills actor Joaquin Phoenix has pulled out of Todd Haynes's new film five days before production was set to begin in Mexico

The film, a gay detective story set in the 1930s, was initiated by the actor as a vehicle for himself. Production company Killer Films is for now left holding the bag

Singer Celine Dion has objected to Donald Trump's unauthorized use of her song "My Heart Will Go On," from *Titanic*, during his campaign rallies

A 26-foot-tall, 15-ton statue of Marilyn Monroe in her *Seven Year Itch* subway-grate pose will be relocated from the front of a Palm Springs art museum to a nearby park. The statue was created in 2011 by Johnson & Johnson heir John Seward Johnson II, who died in 2020

A child in the UK was initially denied a passport because she is named Khaleesi, after a character from *Game of Thrones*. British officials were worried issuing her the document would violate WBD's copyright, which it doesn't. Khaleesi, age 6, and her mother were on their way to Disneyland Paris when officials refused to let them leave for their vacation to the WBD competitor's European theme park

Tinto Brass's 1979 porn-epic *Caligula* will be rereleased to theaters by Drafthouse Films in an "ultimate cut" that adds lots of unused footage, allegedly in a coherent fashion, and has pleased people who appeared in the film, including *Clockwork Orange* actor Malcolm McDowell, but is still not Brass's cut

A piece about *Juno* director Jason Reitman's new film *Saturday Night*, which is about getting the first episode of *Saturday Night Live* on the air, contains the sentence "The levels of authenticity here are staggering"

While on the subject of entertainment journalism, this week I learned that *The Boston Globe* published two puff pieces on the movie *Janet Planet*, but no review

WBD CEO David Zaslav has revealed that the company is worth $9.1 billion less than previously estimated, largely because of the decline in cable TV viewership

Members of Congress are asking that the Justice Department investigate and shut down the proposed Disney / WBD sports streaming service Venu Sports because it is in violation of antitrust laws. The planned charge for the channel is $42.99 a month

For the first time ever, the streaming service Disney+ has posted a profit, and Disney celebrated by raising the cost of a subscription to the channel by $2 per tier. The no-ads tier will now cost $15.99 a month

Disney CEO Bob Iger has promised the film studio will emphasize "quality over quantity" going forward. To that end, he announced the following slate of forthcoming movies: *Toy Story 5*, *Zootopia 2*, *Frozen III*, *Incredibles 3*, *The Mandalorian and Baby Yoda*, *Avatar: Fire and Ash*, *Tron: Ares*, and a live-action version of *Lilo & Stitch*

Disney released a trailer for the live-action version of *Snow White* in which the dwarfs are animated, a further un-little-peopling of American entertainment. This was a compromise, as Disney initially planned to cast the Seven Dwarfs with a motley assortment of actors, six of them not little people, which the media labeled the "diversity dwarfs" when photos from the shoot were leaked last summer

Paramount is firing 15% of its workforce, eliminating about 2,000 jobs, in an attempt to lower costs by $500 million. This after laying off 800 people last February. Many of the cuts will be streaming-service employees

The company has hired Bain & Co. to eventually eliminate $2 billion in annual costs

In addition, Paramount, like WBD, wrote down its value by $6 billion because of a decline in TV revenue

Facebook for some reason has been paying users in India, Vietnam, and the Philippines to make the ugly AI slop that infests their site. These users base the AI rubbish they create on things they learn from YouTube influencers and on Telegram

OpenAI is warning users that they might become addicted ("emotionally reliant") on ChatGPT voice mode, reducing their need for human interaction

The company also revealed that due to a glitch, ChatGPT voice mode may begin speaking to you in your own voice

Blue Velvet director David Lynch has emphysema and announced he can no longer leave his house, so he can't direct on set or on location. He says he may try to direct remotely

August 18, 2024

During a press conference, Republican vice-presidential candidate JD Vance asked rhetorically, "But has anybody ever seen the movie *Gangs of New York*?" before launching into a racist spiel about "ethnic enclaves"

In a panel discussion at the Edinburgh Film Festival, *Rushmore* actor Brian Cox interrupted his tirade against Marvel and DC movies to remind listeners that he was in the 2003 superhero movie *X2: X-Men United*

Litigious *Mr. Nanny* actor Hulk Hogan has warned Ben Affleck and Matt Damon that he will not hesitate to sue them if their movie *Killing Gawker* contains any inaccurate depiction of the ridiculous, sordid mess that is his life

The Landmark Theatres chain of arthouse multiplexes has gone bust and will be auctioned off by New York State, along with other properties owned by real estate developer Charles S. Cohen, of the Cohen Media Group, who has defaulted on a $534 million bank loan. Unclear what this means for other Cohen Media holdings

SAG-AFTRA has made a deal with the AI voice-imitation studio Narrativ to allow the company to replicate actors' voices under certain kinds of deals

Republican presidential candidate Donald Trump is claiming that the large crowds at Democratic presidential candidate Kamala Harris's events are fake, writing on social media that "she 'A.I.'d' it" and that her followers "DIDN'T EXIST!"

A group of critics at the Penske Media publication *IndieWire* have determined that the 2001 Steven Spielberg movie *A.I. Artificial Intelligence* is the best film of the period 2000–2009

Abyss director James Cameron is insulting fans who notice that the 4K discs of *Aliens* and *True Lies* don't look so great. "They need to move out of mom's basement and meet somebody," the auteur said of his adherents, advising them, in time-honored tradition, to "get a life"

A man visiting the prehistoric cave paintings in Andalusia threw water on some of them, erasing large sections of the artworks, causing irreparable harm. He was under the impression that doing so would allow him to get a better photo of the paintings on his phone, and would therefore make them look great on social media

In addition to the damage perpetrated on Spain's cultural heritage, the country's protected natural beauty was also vandalized. Satirist-singer Katy Perry is under investigation for the unauthorized filming of her latest video "Lifetimes" in the Balearic Islands, where production damaged dunes at Ses Salines Natural Park

It has become clear that there is a Walt Disney quote to counter every bad decision and example of wrong thinking at today's Disney Studios. For example, in 1966 Walt wrote this to shareholders: "I'm a born experimenter. To this day, I don't believe in sequels. I can't follow popular cycles; I have to move on to new things. There are many new worlds to conquer"

Disney is innovating, however, in lawsuits. A widower is suing the company because his wife, an NYU doctor, died last October while eating at one of Disney's Florida theme parks' restaurants, after servers insisted her meal was allergen-free

Disney claims the bereaved husband has no case because he signed up for a free one-month trial of Disney+ on his PlayStation in 2019, and the terms of agreement he checked preclude suing the company, as do the terms he agreed to when he used the My Disney Experience app to buy Epcot tickets for the couple's fatal trip

Paramount has now shut down Paramount Television

A *Rosemary's Baby* prequel movie called *Apartment 7A* will debut on Paramount+ in September

Netflix is lowering their ad prices from $65 to $20, an admission that their rates were not competitive, which is to say they were unrealistic. The streamer charges in CPMs, which is cost per thousand views

Halle Berry and Mark Wahlberg star in *The Union*, latest Netflix feature film, but do not kiss in it because, director Julian Farino says, "You've got to think of this as a three-movie idea." Critics and viewers have called *The Union* "cheesy," "generic," "boring," and "depressing"

"Your Song" singer Elton John will be appearing at the New York Film Festival this fall, there to promote a documentary about himself called *Elton John: Never Too Late* that was directed by *If I Stay* helmer R. J. Cutler and John's husband, David Furnish

Oscarologist Sasha Stone, of *Awards Daily* blog, explained she had made a white-power "boo-boo" on the blog's X account when mocking the White Dudes for Harris campaign Zoom event. Advertisers and publicists are now deserting her site, but Stone has become a "MAGA darling"

Harrison Ford's hat—or more accurately, his stunt double's hat—from the 1984 movie *Indiana Jones and the Temple of Doom* has sold at auction for $630,000. At the same auction the ghost costume from the 1996 movie *Scream* sold for $270,900. (My bid was $270,899)

A crew member on the WBD production *Superman* was found dead of a self-inflicted gunshot wound in a vehicle in the parking lot of Trilith Studios near Atlanta, where the film is being made. The news stories in the entertainment press covering this incident describe the unnamed decedent as "a contractor" or as "a female Teamster," and then spend their last three paragraphs naming the actors in the movie along with the producer-director, and retelling *Superman*'s corporate production history

August 25, 2024

While in the UK last week, *Clueless* actor Alicia Silverstone posted a TikTok of herself eating a poisonous fruit she picked from a stranger's garden

Lionsgate, in promoting *Megalopolis*, released a trailer featuring a bunch of fake quotes from movie critics that were meant to illustrate how Francis Ford Coppola's films have grown in reputation since their original releases

Andrew Sarris and Pauline Kael were among the critics whose quotes were generated for this purpose by AI

A consulting publicist named Eddie Egan is to blame for hatching this scheme and coming up with the quotes using AI instead of research

The quotes were not only fictional, but contradicted the critics' original reviews of Coppola's films

The fast-food chain Chick-fil-A is starting a streaming service that will produce scripted content, reality TV shows, and animation. It is set to launch before the end of the year. I've always expected brands to do this, the cost of entry is low, surprised more haven't

Last week Republican presidential candidate Donald Trump was pretending to be opposed to AI. This week he used AI images to erroneously state that *Cats* actor Taylor Swift had endorsed him for president and that her fans were supporting him, too. Now Swift may sue him

Beanie Bubble actor Zach Galifianakis, who once interviewed Barack Obama on his fake TV talk show *Between Two Ferns*, now says that the Democrats are too focused on Hollywood celebrities in their presidential campaigning

"My Kink is Karma" singer Chappell Roan has announced that she has no intention of making a move into film acting, and is turning down all movie offers. Her reasons? Actors are crazy, she gets freaked out by film people, the film industry is scary in general, and making movies is an out-of-control time suck. She concluded her list of valid points by saying maybe she'd do a cameo

Cameo king Benny Safdie will appear in *Happy Gilmore 2*

The *Barbie* team of director-writer Greta Gerwig and star producer Margot Robbie are upset that Mattel may be going forward with an animated *Barbie* movie. They aren't part of the deal, are annoyed the brand is getting away from them, and suspect an animated movie will be, you know, an animated movie

The *New York Times* film critic Alissa Wilkinson this week wrote a whole feature about how she hate-watches TV shows she knows are bad, saying she can't get enough of them. She hate-watches five shows, and admits she can't stop. Evidently there are not enough films to see and write about, or maybe news of them is not getting through to her

The director of *Alien: Romulus*, Fede Álvarez, says that it is "unfair" that the late actor Ian Holm had not been deepfaked using AI to appear in more *Alien* movies before he got the idea to do it. "We did it with a lot of respect," Álvarez says, though no one agrees

Convicted felon and former US Congressman George Santos gave a review of *Alien: Romulus* on the way to jail: "absolutely awful, absolutely terrible, do not waste your time"

Blink Twice director Zoë Kravitz says she had never heard of Jeffrey Epstein until halfway through writing her film, formerly called *Pussy Island*

Amazon MGM has appended a trigger warning to *Blink Twice* that shows before screenings

Snow White and the Huntsman director Rupert Sanders's remake of the 1994 movie *The Crow* has been released to terrible reviews

How can this be, when Sanders says he took inspiration from *Diva*, *Ghost Dog*, *A Matter of Life and Death*, *Stalker*, and *Wings of Desire*?

Pirates of the Caribbean actor Johnny Depp has directed a movie called *Modí, Three Days on the Wing of Madness*. It is not a biopic of Indian prime minister Narendra Modi but a biopic of the painter Amedeo Modigliani. Depp is not in the film, which will premiere at the San Sebastián Film Festival next month

Disney+ has canceled their TV series *Star Wars: The Acolyte* after one season because no one was watching it, even though IP products are infallible moneymakers and audience magnets

Edgar Bronfman Jr., of the Bronfman liquor family, who once owned Universal Studios and is the former head of Warner Music, is now trying to buy Paramount and National Amusements, despite the sale to Skydance seeming to have been a done deal. His bid is lower than Skydance's, and somehow this is all on the up-and-up

A *Salem's Lot* feature-film shot three years ago will debut on Max instead of being deep-sixed by WBD

John Woo's feature film remake of his 1989 masterpiece *The Killer* has debuted on Peacock

The historically landmarked Jay Littleton Ball Park in Ontario, Calif.—built in the 1930s and the shooting location of John Sayles's *Eight Men Out* and Penny Marshall's *A League of Their Own*—has burned to the ground in a fire of unknown origin

Le Samouraï actor Alain Delon, who died the week before last, wanted his dog Loubo euthanized and buried with him. The Brigitte Bardot Foundation has stepped in to prevent the dog's murder, and Loubo will live with Delon's heirs

September 1, 2024

Dark City director Alex Proyas, who made the original 1994 version of *The Crow*, has been roasting the failed and unnecessary remake on social media. He marked himself "Safe from seeing *Crow* 2024" on Facebook, noted the film's poor box office, highlighted brutal reviews, and sarcastically wondered if a French piece calling the film "a gigantic insult" meant that the film was bad

Ocean's Eleven actors George Clooney and Brad Pitt were paid $45 million each to star in *Wolfs*, an Apple Original movie that will debut at the Venice Film Festival, which is happening now, and will next play in theaters for a week this month before heading to Apple TV+

Great Expectations director Alfonso Cuarón told the press at Venice that *Disclaimer*, his TV series for Apple TV+, is really a seven-part movie

At the Venice press conference for his new film *Baby Invasion*, a cigar-smoking Harmony Korine explained that "we're starting to see Hollywood crumble creatively" because it is "so locked in on convention." The *Trash Humpers* director blames Hollywood for ignoring and misusing today's youth, who would, he claims, rather be working in gaming and Twitch streaming than going into filmmaking and acting

During another press conference at Venice, Sigourney Weaver was asked if her role in the *Aliens* movies played a part "in making it possible that a woman like Kamala Harris could become president of the United States"

Weaver took the bait, teared up, and said, "It's true," before regaining her well-known composure and asking for a vodka

The Telluride Film Festival is also going on, in Colorado. This year, it seems the venerable cinephile institution has become an after-party for the Democratic National Convention

Guests this year include Hillary Clinton and James Carville, and fest director Julie Huntsinger gave quotes including the following to the Penske publications *Variety* and *The Hollywood Reporter* and the not-yet-Penske *Los Angeles Times*:

"There's a normalcy that's starting to feel very good again. People want to feel hopeful. Some movies are so powerful they bring you to tears, but as I always say, we reflect what these great filmmakers want to discuss. We want to find a way to move closer to the light"

She continued, "Even if these movies don't get distribution in time for the election, I want everybody to leave here saying, 'My God, I was so moved by this.' I want people to feel more hopeful, more enlightened and more resolute about our ability to make a difference in the world"

And: "There are a lot of musicals and movies with music as an important part of the film, which I believe comes from our relentless desire to be uplifted. We don't want to live in darkness. And film, to me, is always a light. Even in those really difficult ones that make us cry, there's a catharsis that comes out of that"

Bodies Bodies Bodies actor Amandla Stenberg is the latest actress to describe *Star Wars* nuts as a problem. She says their "hyper-conservative bigotry and vitriol, prejudice, hatred, and hateful language" on social media was part of the reason her TV series *Star Wars: The Acolyte* was canceled by Disney+

Charlie's Angels actor Drew Barrymore has posted on Instagram saying she regrets posing for *Playboy* in 1995. "I thought it would be a magazine that was unlikely to resurface because it was paper," she writes in the post, which calls for greater chastity in American pop culture, so that kids won't be brought up like she was, by Hollywood royalty

The Circle actor Tom Hanks warned us this week on Instagram that ads touting wonder drugs and miracle cures that use his face and voice have been made without his consent using AI. "DO NOT BE SWINDLED," he wrote, in all caps

Hanks did not add that Forrest Gump didn't really meet John F. Kennedy, Lyndon Johnson, Bear Bryant, Abbie Hoffman, Vivian Malone Jones, Richard Nixon, and John Lennon, and nor did Gary Sinise really lose his legs in Vietnam

A new horror movie called *AfrAId* (yes, it's supposed to be spelled that way), in which the villain is an AI, has been called the worst movie of the year so far

The new biopic *Reagan*, just released but shot in 2020, was given an all-star premiere this week in Dixon, Ill., at the Dixon Theatre, in operation since 1922 and *Tennessee's Partner* actor Ronald Reagan's hometown movie theater. The film has been called the second-worst of the year

The Apprentice, biopic of young Donald Trump in his Roy Cohn days, has finally received a release date after one of its producers, billionaire Dan Snyder, a Trump supporter, tried to halt it. The film will come out October 11, about a month before the US presidential election in which Trump is the Republican candidate

The New York City real estate market has gotten so tough that *Lean on Pete* actor Chloë Sevigny is on Instagram asking for help finding a sublet in Lower Manhattan

Lone Ranger actor Armie Hammer is selling his 2017 GMC Sierra 1500 Denali pickup truck on CarMax, says he can't afford the gas anymore (23 mpg city / 30 mpg hwy) because he doesn't get enough work since becoming an accused cannibal pariah

A stampede broke out at Disney World in Orlando, Fla., after visitors thought they heard a gunshot and made “active shooter” claims. Large crowds tried to leave the theme park en masse, abandoning baby strollers, while others hid in gift shops, overturning displays and shelves and scattering pricey memorabilia to the floors. The gunshot turned out to be a popping balloon

Daniel Sancho Bronchalo, 30-year-old YouTube chef and son of *Everyone Will Burn* actor Rodolfo Sancho, has received a life sentence in Thailand for murdering and dismembering a Colombian plastic surgeon, Edwin Arrieta Arteaga, after a lover’s spat on the party island Koh Pha Ngan

A chilling story from a subscriber in the UK who took his son to see a revival screening of *Pulp Fiction* at the Odeon Liverpool Switch Island: “I thought I had seen everything vis-à-vis bad behaviour in the cinema but this evening saw a first … Guy two seats away from me was on his phone, I asked him to switch it off … He said just need to do this … Eventually he put it in his pocket … 30 minutes later he leaves … He then returns … He had been ordering Uber Eats … He then opens up what appears to be many courses of a Chinese banquet …”

Next time I’m at the Cinémathèque in Paris, remind me to Uber Eats a Royale with cheese

September 8, 2024

Holy Spider director Ali Abbasi’s Young Trump biopic, *The Apprentice*, is being distributed by Briarcliff Entertainment and has an October 11 release date, but even so the production has taken the unprecedented step of launching a Kickstarter campaign to somehow use the money it raises from the public for "expanded distribution"

In the first day the campaign received about $140,000 against a goal of $100,000, and the pot is growing daily. As of this writing, they've squeezed $265,219 out of 3,915 souls

Executive producer Amy Baer, who is also board president of Women in Film, says, "*The Apprentice* is first and foremost humanist, which makes it radically different than all the political noise"

The trailer for the forthcoming *Minecraft* movie has been released to revulsion from the world's many, many *Minecraft* players, who have called it "embarrassing," "horrendous," "AI-generated," and "drab," and mentioned that the film's star, *Year One* actor Jack Black, looks "depressed" and "disturbing" in it. Predictions claim this will not hurt the film's box office

But now evidently everybody hates Jack Black, who has become the poster boy for the cheap, endless infantilization of American cinema

In TIFF news, start of the opening night film, *Nutcrackers*, starring *Zero Effect* actor Ben Stiller, was interrupted by pro-Palestinian protestors opposed to Royal Bank of Canada, a financial supporter of Israel, being the festival's "official bank partner"

Audience members booed the protestors and shouted "Go home!" and "Go away!" so eager were they to see, without delay, a movie that will open on many screens very soon

Actresses tearing up at festivals became an official trend, as Jamie Lee Curtis and Florence Pugh both cried when speaking after the TIFF premieres of their new movies, *The Last Showgirl* and *We Live in Time*

An on-screen announcement before at least one movie at TIFF asked the audience to "help by minimizing the use of your phone during" screenings

Ticket to Paradise actor George Clooney denies he and Brad Pitt each got $45 million to act in *Wolfs*, says it was "millions and millions less," doesn't say how much exactly, and adds that it would be bad for the industry if people thought salaries were that high

Clooney and Pitt will star in an *Ocean's 14* movie, which Steven Soderbergh will not direct. He'll be replaced with *All Quiet on the Western Front* director Edward Berger, a German

I Am Love director Luca Guadagnino is set to direct a DC Comics movie for WBD. He has been penciled in for a *Sgt. Rock* adaptation

After years of growth, Chinese films are tanking at the Chinese box office, leading *Alien: Romulus* to do even better in China than it did in the US, where it has been a big hit. Chinese film attendance is down 44% this year

Reagan is a hit, overperforming predictions at the box office, garnering a 98% audience-approval score despite terrible reviews

Girl, Interrupted actor Winona Ryder laments that young actors she works with "are just not interested in movies. Like, the first thing say is, is 'How long is it?'"

Bizarre, eyebrowless OpenAI CEO Sam Altman, in an attempt to jump-start another $100 billion funding round, is trying to convince both international investors and the US government to allow him to build a vast system of data centers, turbines, generators, and semiconductor-manufacturing plants that will speed the process of embedding AI into all aspects of US industry and infrastructure, something no one wants

The oddball AI shill is also insisting that his company be allowed to use any and all copyrighted material to train his AI models, because the amount of content available in the public domain is insufficient for his plans to succeed in "meeting the needs of today's citizens," who have demonstrated no need for AI at all

The Disney leaks have revealed the company's financial secrets and strategy plans, and have exposed the personal data of staff and customers, but no one seems interested

A new documentary called *Lover of Men* investigates the possibility that Abraham Lincoln was gay, but the film's poster features Honest Abe with the David Bowie *Aladdin Sane* lightning bolt over his face. Is it because the Great Emancipator is freaking out in a moonage daydream? No, says director Shaun Peterson, it's an attempt to appeal to Gen Z

The ultraconservative MAGA content factory Tenet Media, not named after the Christopher Nolan film, turns out to be a Russian front, paying right-wing influencers (YouTube podcasters) up to $400,000 a month, with $100,000 signing bonuses, along with performance bonuses, to make at least four videos a week extolling their reactionary conspiracy theories and other ultrarightist notions

In his own defense, one of the podcasters, the aptly named Matt Christiansen, asked, "How am I unwittingly duped into saying someone else's words when I wrote every one of them?" How indeed, Matt?

YouTube has removed the Tenet Media accounts

Beetlejuice actor Michael Keaton would like to be referred to and billed as Michael Keaton Douglas going forward. Michael Douglas is his real name, just as *La La Land* actor Emma Stone is really Emily Stone and would now like to be called that

One of the cast members of the new reality TV show *The Secret Lives of Mormon Wives* is Ben Affleck's cousin, Zac Affleck

September 15, 2024

In the forthcoming biopic *Better Man*, about the British pop singer Robbie Williams, Williams is played by a CGI monkey

The corporate-product movie *Cola Wars* has found the perfect team to bring it to the screen: it will be helmed by *Bubble* director Judd Apatow and produced by Steven Spielberg

There is talk there will be a belated sequel to the Spielberg-produced *Goonies* (*Old Goonies*?). The stars of the 1985 original, however, say they've heard nothing about it

Mediocre, bombastic German director Roland Emmerich plans to remake David Lean's 1962 film *Lawrence of Arabia* as a limited TV series called *Lawrence* in *Arabia*. The show will be written by Anthony McCarten, who wrote the botched biopics *Bohemian Rhapsody*, *The Two Popes*, and *Whitney Houston: I Wanna Dance with Somebody*

Matewan actor James Earl Jones has died at 93, but his Darth Vader voice, owned by Disney, will live on through AI, so that it can be used in future *Star Wars* content. Jones approved this decision before his death

A *Hollywood Reporter* headline put it this way: "James Earl Jones' Death Spurs Questions About His 'Star Wars' Future"

Lucasfilm is being sued by the Estate of Peter Cushing for recreating the late actor in the 2016 movie *Rogue One: A Star Wars Story*, in which Cushing's performance as Grand Moff Tarkin was brought back to life despite Cushing's 1994 death

The amount that Meta, Google, Microsoft, and Amazon have spent on AI so far—a combined $52.9 billion—is almost $6 billion more than it would cost to replace all the remaining lead pipes in the US

Hillbilly Elegy director Ron Howard says he is "surprised and concerned" by "rhetoric" from the Trump/Vance campaign. He says the JD Vance biopic he made for Netflix was not political and that he and Vance "didn't talk a lot about politics" when they were making the movie. "I was interested in his upbringing and survival tale," Howard explains

Israeli prime minister Benjamin Netanyahu has failed to block a work-in-progress screening of the documentary *The Bibi Files* at TIFF. The film includes police interviews with Bibi and claims he is prolonging the war in Gaza to avoid facing a possible prison sentence on corruption charges

The film also exposes Netanyahu to bribery charges, and includes *L.A. Confidential* producer Arnon Milchan asking the Israeli police not to use the word "bribery" when discussing his dealings with Netanyahu, as that would make him look bad

Leonard Leo, the Federalist Society lawyer and conservative activist who runs the Marble Freedom Trust, a political advocacy group and "social welfare organization," is vowing to spend $1 billion to "crush liberal dominance" in the entertainment industry, "where left-wing extremism is most evident"

Megalopolis director Francis Ford Coppola is suing the Penske Media publication *Variety* for libel for reporting various stories about the production of the film that are turning out to be less than true. Unclear why other Coppola-smearing Penske products like *The Hollywood Reporter* and *IndieWire* are not part of the suit

WBD stock is at an all-time low this summer, hovering at around $7 a share, while WBD CEO David Zaslav attends high-profile, big-ticket sports events like the US Open, which he went to with *Be Cool* actor John Travolta

Meanwhile, Sony Pictures CEO Tony Vinciquerra says that the film industry is entering a period of chaos that will be defined by bankruptcies, sales, and mergers

The social media site Letterboxd has removed the 1997 animated movie *Neon Genesis Evangelion: The End of Evangelion* from consideration as one of the site's top 250 movies, saying it is merely the last two episodes of a TV series put together. This has annoyed many, many people, including some who are adults

Film critic Jonathan Rosenbaum is selling his entire Blu-ray and DVD collection on Craigslist for $20,000

The forthcoming *Hunt for Gollum* movie, a *Lord of the Rings* sequel, will be split into two movies that will be released separately

Denzel Washington's son Malcolm has made his directorial debut at TIFF with *The Piano Lesson*, from August Wilson's play. A Netflix movie, it was produced by Washington's daughter, Katia, and costars his other son, *Tenet* actor John David

Maddox and Pax, the sons of Angelina Jolie, got jobs on the set of *Without Blood*, a new movie starring *Spy Kids 3-D: Game Over* actor and Instagram content creator Salma Hayek, who says the scions "worked hard." The film premiered at TIFF, where it was called "turgid" and "a big mess"

The pair also worked on *Maria*, in which their mother stars, "in the assistant director department"

One of the drawbacks of doing this newsletter is that every week I have to wade through dozens of headlines about the British royal family to get to legitimate *End Times* news. Now the royals themselves have begun to release filmed propaganda. Out now: a short post-cancer-treatment video that Princess Kate Middleton of Wales hired a filmmaker named Will Warr to direct for her. The fawning press has called the film a "masterstroke"

A runner has died after collapsing due to heat stroke at the finish line of Disneyland's Halloween Half Marathon. Bobby Caleb Graves, 33 or 35, a TikTok personality, had the day before made a TikTok video after passing out from heat exhaustion while walking his dog, saying he was worried about running the race because of the heat wave in California. It should be noted that Halloween is not for another 46 days, but going by the Disney calendar, this year it came sooner for Bobby Graves

Relatedly, it turns out that one of Vladimir Putin's "secret" sons, Ivan, age 9, is a Disney cosplayer

September 22, 2024

Batman has received a star on the Hollywood Walk of Fame. News reporting on the decision emphasizes that Batman is "the first superhero" to receive this honor, not that he doesn't exist

In the lamest, creepiest humblebrag of the year, unfunny actor Josh Gad says he should not have used his real voice in *Frozen*, because babies recognize it in the supermarket

Heard of Instacart, Josh?

An eight- or nine-hour Netflix docuseries on Prince is being blocked from release by the late Purple One's estate over objections to its quality. News reports keep referring to the series simply as "a documentary"

MSNBC news host Rachel Maddow has produced a TV show called *From Russia with Lev*, about Lev Parnas, Russian no-goodnik and Republican Party operative. It's premiering on MSNBC and the news network describes it just as "a documentary"

CNN has made a similar show about Democratic operative James Carville that they are also just calling "a documentary" in the lead-up to its premiere

This week at the Camden Film Festival, the Archival Producers Alliance released official rules for documentary-film producers on how to “navigate the ethical uses of AI.” The alliance does not reject the use of generative AI, instead encouraging four principles be observed: value of primary sources, transparency, legality, and consideration of whether creating human simulations is ethical

I have a counterproposal: turn the conference into a Christopher Guest movie

Speaking of comedy, Monty Python members Eric Idle and John Cleese are in a Twitter feud over Python finances. Idle is upset he still has to work even though he is now 81. When a Twitter user suggested the Pythons license a Netflix documentary to revive interest in their earlier work, Idle responded “Fuck Netflix and fuck documentaries”

According to a new law passed in California, it is now illegal to replace an actor with an AI-generated semblance

At the Fast Company Innovation Festival, Netflix CEO Ted Sarandos has called theatrical release of movies an “inefficient” way to make money

At the same time, Sarandos is insisting that his competitors in the streaming biz release their viewership numbers, despite not releasing real numbers on Netflix’s own movies and shows. Of the pseudodata Netflix does release, Sarandos said, “I don’t think we could be anymore transparent than this”

Also at the Fast Company Innovation Festival, *Deadpool* actor Ryan Reynolds compared collective audience delight at his movies in theaters to “the movement of kelp underwater”

An article in *Rolling Stone* posits that because the new Netflix movie *Uglies*, from *Charlie’s Angels* director McG, is so bad, all subsequent adaptations of young-adult genre fiction should be animated

The stated reason for giving up on humanity here is that live-action cinema is too limiting and that no current directors or studios are imaginative enough to bring "far-reaching, mind-expanding worlds" to the screen without giving the process over to computer animation

Oracle founder Larry Ellison, an 80-year-old billionaire who looks 50, and who owns 98% of the Hawaiian island Lana'i, and who was once the largest owner of private property in Malibu, and whose two children are Hollywood studio owners, says he looks forward to a vast AI-driven surveillance state, because it will ensure citizens are always on their best behavior

The tech giants Google, Microsoft, Meta, and Apple have been a little off in estimating the harmful emissions their data centers generate. By how much? Emissions are 662% higher than they claimed

Disney-Pixar's *Inside Out 2* is the highest-grossing animated movie ever made. Part of the reason is that the studio totally ganked the people who made it, working them like mad and then laying them off so they would not be able to participate in profit sharing when the film hit the $1 billion mark

Production of the film has been described as messy, overtime-driven, and "the largest crunch in the studio's history"

Laid-off employees were asked not to come to the studio to get their belongings, because that might make remaining employees uncomfortable

In addition, employees were tasked with making *Inside Out 2* "less gay," because Disney blames recent theatrical failures on a brief same-sex kiss in 2022's *Lightyear*

Studios shouldn't worry about these disgruntled ex-employees, however. Billionaire media executive Barry Diller, 82, says that once AI is fully in place, of the "hundreds, thousands of people on staff to make animated movies, you're not going to need anyone"

Lionsgate has signed a deal with the AI start-up Runway. This will give the tech company access to Lionsgate's movie library, while in exchange the studio will get a custom AI model they can use to eliminate storyboard artists and special effects crews

At the same time, Runway can use preexisting Lionsgate content to train future AI models, so that Lionsgate can then eliminate more personnel, while Runway strip-mines Lionsgate content to use for other, as yet unannounced purposes

Disney's 2023 live-action reboot of *The Little Mermaid* cost $335.1 million to make—glad they include the .1—most of the budget coming from the use of CGI to create the animated fish and other underwater creatures, and has to date lost about $5 million, though because of streaming it is impossible to tally exactly how much

The CGI in the movie has been described as "eerie," "off-putting," "contorted," and "unnatural"

Says Disney CEO Bob Iger, "while we are extremely proud of what's on screen, it's gotten to a point where it's extraordinarily expensive"

Lazarus Effect actor Donald Glover says *Star Wars* isn't fun anymore, but he will change that when he plays Lando Calrissian again, in the forthcoming movie *Lando*. "We have a responsibility to have an enjoyment," Glover explains, in a way that already makes it sound fun

Google has announced it will offer an AI feature inside YouTube so that users can make six-second AI shorts

Official UK director Danny Boyle is making *28 Years Later*, belated sequel to his 2002 fast-zombie movie *28 Days Later*, using only an "adapted iPhone 15 Pro Max" smartphone, including scenes shot with the phone attached to farm animals

A new German movie, *Traumnovelle*, based on the same Arthur Schnitzler novella as Stanley Kubrick's *Eyes Wide Shut*, includes a fully AI-generated dream sequence that's been described as "incongruous"

Director of the film is Florian Frerichs, a German

Christian Tafdrup, Danish director of the original, 2022 version of new Hollywood horror movie *Speak No Evil*, says the remake is safe and sanitized, with the American obsession with family solidarity and winning firmly in place. Tafdrup says we should be traumatized at the movies, not cheer at the end. His version finishes with the lead couple being stoned to death in a ditch

Bollywood director-writer-actor Soham Shah claims in a lawsuit that his 2009 movie *Luck* is the basis for the Netflix TV series *Squid Game*, somehow forgetting that everybody already knows *Squid Game* was directly ripped off from the 2000 Kinji Fukasaku movie *Battle Royale*

A low-budget conservative comedy-documentary, *Am I Racist?*, made by the right-wing political commentator Matt Walsh in the style of Michael Moore, has opened on 1,500 screens in cineplexes across the country, and has been ignored by mainstream movie reviewers

The studio making it is Walsh's co-right-wing commentator Ben Shapiro's Daily Wire

As long as the majors make so few films, movies like *Am I Racist?* and *Reagan*, made by right-wing and Christian studios, will leap in to the fill the void left in multiplexes without enough movies for their screens

The National Association of Theatre Owners (NATO), which includes the chains AMC, Regal, and Cinemark, has pledged to spend $2.2 billion—the .2 will make the difference—on theater upgrades in the next few years. The organization has found that today's audiences complain of dirty auditoriums, broken seats, and substandard projection. Their solution? Add higher-end dining experiences, pickleball courts, and ziplines

This is also an admission that the cineplexes think they have too many screens and want to use that real estate for other things

The UK Home Office has denied another child a passport over their bizarre interpretation of copyright law. This time a little kid named Loki Skywalker Mowbray—young son of two British soldiers—was refused a passport over the name Skywalker, use of which officials said violated a Disney trademark. (Loki was fine?) The name doesn't violate any law, but the family was told they would need Disney's permission to have it included on Loki Skywalker's documentation, and until then, nobody leaves Blighty

Did you know that last year two totally different and separate movie versions of the Henry James novella *The Beast in the Jungle* were brought to the screen in France? One was Bertrand Bonello's *The Beast*, the other uses the full title and was directed by Patric Chiha and cowritten with Axelle Ropert. Why now, Frenchies?

Star David Harbour insists that the forthcoming Marvel movie *Thunderbolts* is "comic-book accurate"

September 29, 2024

The Penske press is gloating that Francis Ford Coppola's *Megalopolis* has debuted at the box office behind an Indian movie, the Telugu action-drama *Devara: Part 1*

Which, in turn, *Variety* calls a "scattered, excruciating mess"

The Three Mile Island nuclear power plant in Londonderry, Pa., that melted down in 1979 and closed in 2019, will reopen in 2028 under a twenty-year contract to supply power to Microsoft's AI data centers

True Lies director James Cameron has joined the board at Stability AI, stating he predicted how harmful AI would be when he made *The Terminator* in 1984, then adding "I warned you"

Which is kind of like Smith & Wesson telling you that guns are dangerous and then finding you forty years later and shooting you with an AR15

As it lays off journalists and other staff, and shuts down presses, the *Evening Standard* newspaper in London will use AI to revive art critic Brian Sewell, who died in 2015 at age 84, so the Sewell-bot can review new art shows

After last week's spate of AI rationalizations from octogenarian Hollywood machers (Larry Ellison, Barry Diller), it is becoming clearer whom AI is for

The New York Film Festival, which opened this week, partners with Bloomberg Philanthropies, an organization that provides direct support for settlement infrastructure in the West Bank and denies Palestinians basic rights. Filmmakers showing films in the festival this year are calling for the fest to sever ties with Bloomberg Philanthropies and any other funders who support war crimes in Gaza, and urging the fest to make a statement calling for a ceasefire

Signatories include film directors Jem Cohen, Mike Leigh, Julia Loktev, Guy Maddin, and Athina Rachel Tsangari

The day the film *No Other Land* press screened for the festival, the home of its codirector, Basel Adra, was invaded by Israeli soldiers, and his father was bound, blindfolded, and kidnapped, then held against his will at a settlement outpost

Netflix's forthcoming TV series remake *East of Eden* is opening new vistas in nepotism, by having *Ruby Sparks* actor Zoe Kazan as its showrunner and writer. Kazan is the granddaughter of Elia Kazan, who made the 1955 movie adaptation of the John Steinbeck novel, starring James Dean, who had no children

20th Century Studios will produce a belated remake of Curtis Hanson's 1992 psycho-thriller *The Hand That Rocks the Cradle*

Argentinian director Lisandro Alonso will make a sequel to his 2001 film *La Libertad*, to be called *La Libertad Doble*. I suspect this story got reported only because it had the word "sequel" in it

Finally, inevitably, there will be a pickleball comedy starring Ben Stiller

An article in *The Daily Beast* celebrating the 30th anniversary of overrated movie *The Shawshank Redemption* this week was headlined "*Shawshank Redemption*'s 'River of Shit' Was Full of Actual Poop"

The poop appears in paragraph 19 of the piece, which is 22 paragraphs long and is otherwise a standard appreciation of the film

Other depressing, confusing, trivializing, and/or foreboding headlines this week:

"*Paddington in Peru* Will Nod to Werner Herzog's *Aguirre* and *Fitzcarraldo*"

"Hacker Plants False Memories in ChatGPT to Steal User Data in Perpetuity"

"*Megalopolis* Records One of Adam Driver's Lowest-Ever Rotten Tomatoes Ratings"

Reporting on the growing sexual harassment accusations against the late British Egyptian billionaire Mohamed al-Fayed—a businessman who owned a department store, a hotel, and a soccer team, and who had no connection at all to the entertainment industry or showbiz—has been appearing exclusively in the entertainment section of the news. Why? Maybe because he was on *Da Ali G Show* once?

A team of con men in Spain impersonating *Babel* actor Brad Pitt online has scammed two women out of about $350,000. The five fake Brads who were arrested had contacted victims through an online fan page, then DM'd and emailed them, somehow fooling them into thinking they were communicating with the *Snatch* actor himself. At that point the false Pitt explained he needed money and asked them to transfer it to him in large sums

October 6, 2024

It's been only a week since *The New York Times* and *Entertainment Weekly* (not a weekly) were bombarding us with headlines like "Coppola's *Megalopolis* Plays to Near-Empty Theaters" and "*Megalopolis* Suffers an Apocalypse Bow." Why does it feel like a lifetime ago?

The Headline of the Week, however: "I Saw the Controversial New Demi Moore Thriller About Women's Bodies and Ugh, Hard Relate"

Relatedly, an *Independent* article headlined "The Extreme Body Horror Film Causing Mass Cinema Walkouts Around the World: The Movie Is Even Shocking Those Who Aren't Easily Rattled" turns out to be a series of social media quotes from people at screenings of *The Substance* who saw other people walking out

Similarly, reports also in the British press about massive walk-outs during the first scene of *Terrifier 3*, in which a family is murdered, turn out to be from one projectionist (in this case, a theater worker who sells candy, has to wear a uniform, and starts the DCP machine) who "heard they happened"

The British magazine *Total Film* is closing after 27 years and 356 issues

Democratic California governor Gavin Newsom has vetoed a bill that would have held AI companies responsible for any harm their products might cause or create

Ubiquitous AI startup Runway is offering filmmakers up to $1 million if they agree to use AI when making their movies

Meta has announced its own AI product, called Movie Gen, a video generator that "adds sounds"

An AI museum, the first, will open in Los Angeles in 2025. It will be called Dataland and will be housed in the shopping center in the Gehry-designed Grand LA, a hotel and condo complex in downtown Los Angeles. The museum is the "brainchild of Refik Anadol" and will use "ethical data-gathering" for the pieces the museum exhibits, which will evidently also all be Anadol brainchildren

The Walt Disney Company has laid off more employees. This time, the third this year, 75 people in their news division at ABC have been let go

It has been revealed that cop New York Mayor Eric Adams, recently indicted for taking bribes from the government of Turkey, made a cameo appearance in a 2017 Turkish romantic comedy called *Fairytale of New York*, in which he asks characters for political favors

Martin Scorsese had planned to begin shooting twin biopics this year, on Jesus and Frank Sinatra, but they have been postponed for unknown reasons. Scorsese's documentary on ancient shipwrecks off the coast of Sicily will begin shooting in the summer

Before a screening of *Top Gun: Maverick* with a full orchestra at the Royal Albert Hall last week, Tom Cruise gave a short lecture on the history of film music, focusing on the use of "leitmotifs"

Us actor Lupita Nyong'o damaged her vocal cords during her four-day recording session for *The Wild Robot*, in which she voices the lead character. Foregoing surgery, she says she healed it by "just shutting up for three months"

Nick Cave recorded a medley of songs for *Joker: Folie à Deux* that includes "What the World Needs Now Is Love," "Slap That Bass," and "Get Happy"

How to Be Single actor Rebel Wilson has directed a movie called *The Deb*, and is now suing its producers and others for, among other things, not getting it into the Toronto Film Festival

In the Name of the Father actor Daniel Day-Lewis is coming out of his early retirement, which began in 2017, to act in a movie directed by his son, Ronan. The film is called *Anemone*, and the elder Day-Lewis also cowrote it

Nope actor Daniel Kaluuya will be honored with a statue in London's Leicester Square, result of a poll of 50,000 British film fans. Other statutes in the area include Harry Potter, Batman, Wonder Woman, Mary Poppins, and Gene Kelly, a real person like Kaluuya

The 007, a pop-up theme bar dedicated to the fictional character James Bond, has opened up in London's Burlington Arcade. It features memorabilia from Bond movies, and closes December 31 this year

There will be a remake of *Creature from the Black Lagoon*, directed by James Wan

There will be an *Anaconda* reboot, starring—guess who?—Jack Black

Smile director Parker Finn says his *Possession* remake will be "completely bonkers," acknowledges that people who loved the original "might be a little suspect of a remake"

Anne Hathaway has waved the flag of surrender and will be appearing in both *Princess Diaries 3* and *The Devil Wears Prada 2*

Paramount is developing a "live-action" *Rugrats* movie in which the babies will be CGI

Netflix has just released something else no one wanted, a prequel to *The Platform* called *The Platform 2*

The Penske publication *Variety* is finally saying it out loud, asking this week, "Is Disney bad at *Star Wars*?"

Hollywood is battling toxic fans, says *Variety*. These bullies, often racists, pester studios via social media about casting and plot points. The solution, say the studios, is to not provoke these unwell people in the first place. To that end, they are now "assembling specialized clusters of superfans" to assess new material. Assessors assemble!

The New York Times asks, "Can a Neon Blue Gummy Worm Cocktail Save the Movies?," referring to a novelty drink AMC theaters made available called a Sandworm Slayer

They didn't ask me, but let me answer that question anyway. First, remember, the problem with film exhibition, as far as the industry is concerned, is never the quality of the movies, the quality of the projection, the high ticket prices, the high food and beverage prices, or the lack of staff and the self-serve concession stands. No, the problem is the audience, who, research doesn't show, is presumed to have bizarre longings for things like novelty drinks, porno popcorn buckets, party rooms, video game arcades, virtual reality headsets, and ziplines. None of which has moved the needle on attendance a whit. So, to answer *The New York Times*, no, a neon-blue gummy-worm cocktail will not save the movies

Shazam! actor Zachary Levi has endorsed Donald Trump for president, calling it career suicide. This after appearing in *Harold and the Purple Crayon*

During a rally in Pennsylvania, after Republican candidate for president Donald Trump expressed interest in establishing "one real rough, nasty" and "violent day," in order to end crime, or maybe just "one rough hour, and I mean real rough," during which the police would be allowed to combat lawbreaking with unrestrained force, *The Purge* began trending on social media

Rust will have its world premiere in November at the prestigious Camerimage International Film Festival in Poland, in honor of Halyna Hutchins, the cinematographer shot and killed on the set

Kill Dil actor and Hindu ultranationalist political leader Govinda accidentally shot himself in the leg last week, while leaving his home in Mumbai at 4:45 a.m. to catch a flight, and the Bollywood press is speculating both that it was a suicide attempt and a publicity stunt

October 13, 2024

Greetings, my friend. You are interested in the unknown, the mysterious, the unexplainable. That is why you are here. We are all interested in the future, for that is where you and I are going to spend the rest of our lives.

Apple TV+ will now be available on Amazon Prime, as streaming continues to flounder and become cable TV

There are not enough rom-coms made, even though there is a large market for warm, funny films about relationships starring relatable, endearing actors. So Netflix is jumping in with one starring Sacha Baron Cohen and Rosamund Pike

Last Christmas director Paul Feig is surprised his Amazon action-comedy starring mismatched duo (except in annoyance) John Cena and Awkwafina has been lambasted by critics and has no word of mouth. However, *Jackpot!*, which came out August 15, is the No. 1 movie on Amazon Prime. Feig says he is "getting the last laugh" on critics, who called his movie "feeble" and "grating"

Protestors interrupt screenings at the New York Film Festival: pro-Palestinian protestors during a Q&A with Pedro Almodóvar for his new film *The Room Next Door* and climate advocates during Paul Schrader's new one, *Oh, Canada*. Almodóvar invited the protestors onstage to state their case. Schrader has already made *First Reformed*

The protestors also announced, "We have respect for the arts"

People in New York City have been waiting up to three hours to get photographed inside the Criterion Closet van holding up Blu-rays of *House* and *The Battle of Algiers*

WBD superhero comic book sequel-musical *Joker: Folie à Deux* is a big bomb with critics and audiences

Director Todd Phillips says he meant for that to happen

The Penske press is reporting that Phillips refused to liaise with WBD's DC Comics division in making the movie, the idea for which came to Joaquin Phoenix in a dream. Like those are bad things

J:FÀD opening box office was lower than the previous two lowest comic book movie openings, *Morbius* (2022) and *The Marvels* (2023)

WBD stock remains at an all-time low as, once again, like last year, the company has put out one of the year's biggest successes, *Dune: Part Two*, and a giant bomb that erased all its profits. (Last year it was *Barbie* and *The Flash*)

Purportedly "plenty of soul-searching is taking place on the Burbank lot." I'll let you know if they find one

WBD has also announced that *Juror #2*, which Clint Eastwood has announced is his final film and which did well in trailer tests, will open in only 50 theaters November 1, then go to streaming two weeks later. *Joker: Folie à Deux* opened in 4,102 theaters

Qantas Flight GF59 from Sydney to Haneda had an entertainment-system malfunction before takeoff that would only allow one movie to be shown on all screens aboard the plane. The passengers were asked to vote for which movie it would be and chose *Daddio*, starring Dakota Johnson and Sean Penn. It turned out to be "an inappropriate movie" that they didn't understand would be "racy," and also "there was no way to turn it off." Eventually the crew switched the film to an unnamed children's movie

The new movie *White Bird* is both a sequel and a prequel to the 2017 Julia Roberts movie *Wonder*. Who knew? About either of these movies

The house in which *Poltergeist* (1982) was shot has been retro-fitted to look like it did in the movie, and is now available to be Airbnb'd

The right-wing movie *Am I Racist?* is now the highest-grossing documentary of the 2020s

In his new memoir *Sonny Boy*, Al Pacino describes almost dying of COVID in 2020. The *Scarecrow* actor says he visited Hamlet's "undiscovered country from whose bourn no traveler returns," calling it "strange porridge" (evidently not a phrase from Shakespeare). Asked if the near-death experience changed his life, the *Cruising* actor said, "Not at all"

Sad and Unfortunate Headlines of the Week:

"*Winne-the-Pooh: Blood and Honey 2* Ending Explained"

"*Disclaimer* IS an Addictive Reminder That Nothing's Ever as It Seems"

"It's Not Just Saoirse Ronan's Job to Make an Addiction Drama Look This Easy—It's Her Passion"

"11 Menendez Brothers Documentaries to Watch After *Monsters*"

"Prince William's Plea for More *Bourne* Films Leaves Director Unmoved"

Grand Budapest Hotel actor Saoirse Ronan also says, "I can't see myself doing Marvel," quickly adding "there's nothing wrong with [those movies] and I think they're brilliant films"

A new fake trailer for *Princess Mononoke* (1997) was made using AI by a man named Pj Accetturo, CEO of a company called FilmPortal.ai. His goal was to make the film look more realistic. The trailer has been deleted because it disgusted the entire planet

Skyfall director Sam Mendes says Amazon / MGM and Eon Productions, who make the James Bond films, want directors "who are more controllable." "They want slightly more malleable people," he continued

There is so much in that "slightly"

Box office in China is now said to be down 23% this year, a signal to Hollywood it plans to ignore

A very long article in *The New York Times* called "How Everyone Got Lost in Netflix's Endless Library" concluded that 0% interest rates allowed Netflix to make a lot of content, which fooled "everyone" into watching tons of it and thinking they liked it

The Pharrell Williams Lego biopic-documentary *Piece by Piece* includes Lego re-creations of the George Floyd protests

The Errol Morris documentary *Separated*, about Trump's family-separation border policy, is being withheld till after the election by NBCUniversal and MSNBC. Morris is surprised the company that gave Donald Trump a reality TV show for 15 years would do this to him

The distributors of the Young Trump biopic *The Apprentice* hired an airplane to cruise over a Trump rally in Pennsylvania flying a banner that read TRUMP GO SEE *THE APPRENTICE* FRIDAY

The British Film Institute has apologized to producer Faisal A. Qureshi for discriminating against him in funding matters because of his name, adding that they are an organization that "cares deeply" about not being perceived as racist

Disney World employees in Orlando, Fla., were pressured to stay at work as Hurricane Milton hit, while at the same time Disney raised theme park ticket prices above "the $200 barrier"

WGA members are being told not to write for Millennium Films, producers of the *Expendables* movies, because they don't pay on time

Ridiculous Hollywood couple Ashton Kutcher and Mila Kunis say they want to move to Europe because Kutcher is upset his various interactions with indicted sex offender Sean "Diddy" Combs keep getting mentioned in the press. "Hollywood is a cesspool," says the *What Happens in Vegas* star

October 20, 2024

Dark City director Alex Proyas, never shy, has pointed out on Twitter that Tesla has ripped off his 2004 movie *I, Robot* for the design of its new Tesla Bot, which is named Optimus, a name from the *Transformers* movies, mixing things up further. The Tesla Bot is an AI-powered robot designed to do human tasks that are "dangerous, repetitive and boring," including ignoring the serial comma rule

Denis Villeneuve, whose *Dune* films feature lots and lots of computer-generated images, says he will "absolutely miss the collective art of creativity, which is so beautifully human" that is cinema, if "one day" movies are made "just with a computer"

Another French Canadian director, Xavier Dolan, the former enfant terrible now age 35, has announced he is ending his self-imposed retirement to make a new horror movie set "in 1985 in the world of the elite." It will be his first film since 2019's *Matthias & Maxime*. Dolan says his main career disappointment was that "certain collaborations" did not lead "to more generosity, or inventiveness," and now realizes that "you have to come to terms with certain decisions that have had an impact on the depth, or lack of depth, of certain films"

Nutcrackers, the Ben Stiller comedy that for some reason opened the Toronto International Film Festival this year, will make its debut November 29 … on Hulu

In another brilliant management move, David Zaslav's Warners Bros. has apologized to *Dark Knight* director Christopher Nolan for screwing up the 2020 release of his film *Tenet* by cutting him "a seven-figure check" and asking him to come back to WBD. Nolan has cashed the check and decided to stick with Universal for his next movie

The Day the Earth Blew Up: A Looney Tunes Movie has been abandoned by Warners, longtime home to the signature *Looney Tunes* animated shorts, and the film will be instead distributed by something called Ketchup Entertainment

Another Reagan movie is in the works. *Reykjavik* will tell the story of the 1986 US-USSR summit in Iceland, will star *Dumb and Dumber* actor Jeff Daniels as the Great Communicator, *I Shot Andy Warhol* actor Jared Harris as Gorbachev, *American Splendor* actor Hope Davis as Nancy

The Guardian has deleted their review of the documentary *One Day in October* after complaints that it was pro-Israel and unfair to Gazans. The review's writer, Stuart Jeffries, criticized the film for "demonizing" Palestinians as "killers or looters." Director Dan Reed scolded the newspaper for deep-sixing the four-star review

The documentary *Undercover: Exposing the Far Right* has been pulled from the BFI London Film Festival over "security concerns" for festival workers. Fest director Kristy Matheson calls her decision "heartbreaking," adding that "the film is incredibly important and we wish it the best"

Union (not to be confused with the Netflix mockbuster *The Union*), a documentary on union organizing at an Amazon warehouse, won an award at Sundance but no distributor will release it, so filmmakers Brett Story and Stephen Maing will distribute it themselves

About a Hero (terrible title) is a new documentary opening at IDFA (not to be confused with IDGAF) about one man's challenge to prove Werner Herzog wrong by making an entirely AI-generated film as good as one of Herzog's. A better title would've been *Why*?

Headlines of the Week:

"*Terrifier 3* Is No. 1 Clown"

"Gandalf Involved in 'Most' New *Lord of the Rings* Film Ideas"

"New Horror Debuts with Near-Perfect Rotten Tomatoes Score Despite Causing Vomiting"

As *Longlegs* director Osgood Perkins's new film *The Monkey* comes out, and *LOL* director Joe Swanberg begins making a movie called *Monkey's Magic Merry Go Round*, we are detecting a movement from clowns to monkeys

Along those lines, with *Smile 2* now out, and at least two new films about catfishing and others about "toxic fandom," the combination of fake smiles, lying online, and stanning is now getting the treatment it deserved five years ago

Jack Nicholson's son, Ray, by the way, is in *Smile 2*, being exploited there for his resemblance to his father in *The Shining*

Baywatch actor Priyanka Chopra's mother, Madhu, says that "*nepotism* is a word coined by frustrated people." In actuality it is a word coined in the 15th century when Pope Sixtus IV began granting lucrative favors to his nephews

In response to the Trump campaign using clips from Stanley Kubrick's antiwar film *Full Metal Jacket* in a campaign video to say he was against having "a woke military," Kubrick's red-pilled daughter Vivian responded on social media, at length, to claim her father would have been a Trump supporter, that use of the clip was justified, and that, though it seemed incongruous to say so, the clip would help the cause of freedom. She ended with the single-sentence question, "Capisce?"

Donald Trump has called the makers of *The Apprentice*, the Young Trump biopic now in theaters, "HUMAN SCUM," in all caps, which we can only hope will be the title of the sequel

John Miller, a former NBC marketing executive who worked on Donald Trump's reality TV show *The Apprentice*, has apologized for elevating Trump into the presidency by fabricating his on-screen persona and boardroom, then promoting it all as real

Martin Scorsese is producing a new Beatles documentary for Disney+. Called *Beatles '64*, it features never-seen-before Maysles footage and comes out next month. Can you even call yourself a film director at this point if you've never made a Beatles movie? I hope Vera Drew makes one called *The People's Beatles*

Elaine May needs a "shadow director" for insurance purposes in order to make her new film *Crackpot*, which is to star *A Different Man* actor Sebastian Stan and *Madame Web* actor Dakota Johnson

Telugu director Venky Atluri says of his new film *Lucky Baskhar*, "Everyone who loves money will connect with it"

The Boondock Saints 3 to begin filming this spring, says actor Sean Patrick Flanery

A French play "inspired by *Showgirls*" will open in the Crossing the Line Festival in Manhattan

There is a remake of *Street Trash* coming out that takes place in South Africa. Didn't know you could get Tenafly Viper in Cape Town

Challengers director Luca Guadagnino has been tapped by Lionsgate to helm a remake of *American Psycho*. His 2018 remake of *Suspiria*, by his own account, "made absolutely nothing, it was a disaster at the box office," and was also 53

minutes longer than the original, so of course he is the perfect choice for this

Fan Bingbing, movie star exiled from the screen for five years by the Chinese government for tax evasion in a "yin-yang contract" scheme, is back in a new film, *Green Night*, a Hong Kong–produced lesbian neo-noir thriller. Her last social media post about her film career read, "Without the good policies of the party and the state, without the love and protection of the people, there would be no Fan Bingbing"

Disney and Pixar animator Bolhem Bouchiba is on trial in France for allegedly paying to have underage girls in the Philippines assaulted and raped via livestream. The girls were ages 3 to 15 and Bouchiba allegedly paid for about a thousand children to be "targeted." Bouchiba was the head animator on *Tarzan*, and worked on the following films: *Runaway Brain*, *The Hunchback of Notre Dame*, *Hercules*, *Lilo & Stitch*, *Ratatouille*, *The Incredibles*, *Up*, *Soul*, *Luca*, and *Elemental*. He had been convicted in 2014 of sexually assaulting his partner's daughter, received a suspended sentence, then moved back to France

Five of the top ten box office movies right now are animated—a first (though one of them is a rerelease of *The Nightmare Before Christmas*)

Star Wars actor Harrison Ford has claimed that he acted "like an idiot for money" in the forthcoming *Captain America: Brave New World*, but that he also continues to appear in movies because he gets "essential human contact" from it

WBD DC studio head James Gunn has a dog named Ozu

October 27, 2024

Your guide to lighter Halloween viewing and overlooked spooky-season gems

In an interview with Evgeny Lebedev, the Russian oligarchish owner of London's *Evening Standard* newspaper, *Fate of the Furious* actor Helen Mirren told readers, "I always say it's so sad that Kurt Cobain died when he did, because he never saw GPS." Did she mean GBH?

Eat Pray Love actor James Franco is back, appearing in Rome to promote a new Italian movie he stars in, *Hey Joe*, and "wearing a chocolate-brown hoodie he proudly says he co-designed." Franco has another new movie out, *The Price of Money: A Largo Winch Adventure*, only showing in Europe, so here in the US we won't be able to find out what the price of money is

Elisabeth Murdoch, daughter of Rupert, almost bought the Criterion Collection, which she planned to supplement with "prestige shows" to attract "upscale streaming subscribers"

Disney has a new chairman of the board. It's Morgan Stanley CEO James Gorman, no doubt a "big movie guy" like they all are

WBD will not report box office numbers for *Juror #2*, Clint Eastwood's new (and possibly final) film, which opens in only 50 theaters on November 1

Chick-fil-A streaming service Chick-fil-A Play will launch on November 18. The fast-food streamer plans to offer animated shows, scripted podcasts, cooking shows, and interactive stories—all the cheap things no one wants

Dream Scenario actor Nicolas Cage is anti-AI, warning young actors just graduating about its destructive capacity. "This technology wants to take your instrument.... Consider what I am calling MVMFMBMI: my voice, my face, my body, my imagination—my performance. Protect your instrument," he says

Other actors, including Julianne Moore, Kevin Bacon, and Rosario Dawson, are also warning about AI this week, issuing an open letter decrying the use of their work to train generative AI models, a problem that the SAG and WGA strikes last year predictably did not solve

Adobe says that artists must embrace AI or risk being "left behind," and will not release any new products without AI "enhancements," despite calls from artists to do so

Disney will announce a massive AI initiative aimed at transforming its creative output with an initial focus, of course, on VFX and postproduction

Sony CEO Tony Vinciquerra insists once again that film and television production will have to leave the US for cheaper overseas deals because of rising costs

Writer Nicole LaPorte has a new piece in *The Ankler* about studio bosses saying WFH (work from home) is killing Hollywood

Workers at doc-producer RadicalMedia (one word for some reason) are attempting to unionize

Alcon Entertainment, producer of unnecessary *Blade Runner* sequel *Blade Runner 2049*, is suing Elon Musk and Tesla over AI-generated robotaxi images, which also feature a Ryan Gosling lookalike

Nina actor Zoe Saldaña says she would like to reshoot her scenes in the *Avengers* movies, while also calling the Russo brothers "excellent filmmakers"

Marvel Studios' *Blade* reboot has been postponed once again

There will be a fourth *Spider-Man* movie with Tom Holland

The new *Star Wars* movie has lost its third screenwriter, causing some fans to worry that this particular thousand-year reich may be ending, though a *Mandalorian and Baby Yoda* movie is slated for 2026 release. Lucasfilm is now "actively talking with potential screenwriters," so if you are a potential screenwriter, let them know

German director Edward Berger says he will not make a new *Bourne* movie if there's no "good reason"

Doctor Sleep director Mike Flanagan will make an 8-episode TV miniseries version of *Carrie* for Amazon

Alien: Romulus is being released on VHS in a panned & scanned version. I did not know that the film is an "interquel"

The UK Home Office, as we have seen, loves to deny passports to children it believes have names copyrighted by American entertainment conglomerates. They did not have any qualms this week, however, when they issued a real passport to fictional character Paddington Bear, as a promotion for the forthcoming *Paddington* sequel

The *Gladiator II* popcorn bucket is shaped like the Colosseum and features "augmented reality," with a QR code at the bottom of the container that leads to a scene of gladiators fighting, the grease on their bodies like the popcorn grease on your hand

A new Buzz Lightyear action figure retails for $600

The Penske press has noticed that Lionsgate has released seven flops in a row this year—*Borderlands*, *The Crow*, *Never Let Go*, *The Killer's Game*, *Megalopolis*, *White Bird*, and one called *1992*—noting also that that's not reason enough to oust motion picture chairman Adam Fogelson

Lionsgate has a fix for their predicament, they think: stage adaptations of *La La Land*, *Dirty Dancing*, and *The Hunger Games*

Death of Stalin director Armando Iannucci has adapted *Dr. Strangelove* into a West End play starring *Ruby Sparks* actor Steve Coogan in at least one of the Peter Sellers roles

Pussycat Doll Nicole Scherzinger is the new Norma Desmond in *Sunset Boulevard* on Broadway. *People* magazine writer Dave Quinn says that Desmond would "make a fantastic Real Housewife of Beverly Hills"

Flamin' Hot director Eva Longoria has received the National Medal of the Arts from President Biden

November 10, 2024

WBD CEO David Zaslav has got his biggest wish, and now a regulation-unfriendly administration will take power in Washington, allowing him to achieve his dreams of media consolidation, dreams he seemed to think the other party, if elected, would have stopped or interfered with. There was no evidence of that

You will recall that Zaslav mentioned a few months back that consolidation is what he hoped for. Now the man in charge of Warner Bros. and to a certain extent the future of film production in Hollywood says that the incoming Trump administration will provide "an opportunity for consolidation" that might "provide a real positive and accelerated impact on this industry … that is in generational disruption"

The reason consolidation is needed in the biz, according to Zas, is that it will allow "the best content to win" and "much needed modernization of the regulations," which in turn will make "these businesses stronger," and lead to a "better consumer experience"

It might have been added that the film industry in Hollywood is in generational disruption because of men like Zaslav. WBD revenue is down another 17%, and WBD theatrical revenue has fallen 40% since *Barbie*'s success the summer before last

What is up instead of down for WBD? TV ad revenue, which increased 30%

Zaslav and WBD buried the release of Clint Eastwood's *Juror #2*, which the company opened in only about 50 theaters for a two-week prestreaming awards-qualification run

I saw it in a theater while I could, in my case the Alamo Drafthouse in Brooklyn, which is frowsier and more greasy-smelling than ever, which goes with its decorating scheme, dominated by a sickly orange the color of the fake butter in movie-theater popcorn

Juror #2 was excellent, a final shot at American hypocrisy from a great director who has largely beat the system at its own game.

But in thinking about it I can imagine a different ending more in tune with the week that was

In my ending, the innocent man accused of malice murder is not only found guilty and sentenced to death but is also executed by the State of Georgia. The Nicholas Hoult character, the juror of the title, does nothing to stop the execution, despite being the actual guilty party in the homicide, choosing to go on with his perfect little family life instead of taking responsibility for his actions, as he does in Eastwood's movie *before* the execution can take place. But in my imagined version, it is only *after* the execution that the district attorney played by Toni Collette discovers the truth, when it is *too late*

I saw *Conclave* at a huge cineplex outside of Hartford, Conn. It was a weeknight showing and surprisingly well attended, an almost full theater. The movie's screenplay was good and Edward Berger's direction was moody and fairly concise, aided in no small part by Ralph Fiennes's excellent performance in the lead role. Somehow the German director Berger has become much better at his job since his abysmal 2022 version of *All Quiet on the Western Front*, an inept Netflix movie made to win awards

The ending of *Conclave* presents us with a new version of the kind of film where a character who is a member of an oppressed minority magically appears to set things right. In this case, the character is not only an example of that but also a literal savior figure, being the new pope and all, who just might become the light of the world and bring peace to mankind

In another light, the dark antimatter light of this week's presidential election, *Conclave* becomes an item from an era that *didn't happen.* Instead of being a further extension of liberal feel-goodism in awards-bait filmmaking, it is now an obsolete example of a movie from the brief Harris Era, which lasted from the day Joe Biden dropped out of the race until last Tuesday

Conclave now exists in a twilight that's as strange and dated as the weird, cloistered, airless proceedings in the film itself, defined by self-serving political intrigue, dramatic displays of concern about people's moral behavior, and corrupt infighting among an elite corps of aging men who are out of touch with daily reality

November 17, 2024

Late Autumn extravaganza double issue

In response to a petition calling for equity and inclusion, Poland's prestigious Camerimage Film Festival released a statement in a cinematography magazine in which festival director Marek Zydowicz called for unity and stated that all films shot by women cinematographers in 2023 were mediocre

The festival opened last week and featured the premiere of *Rust,* the movie on which *Pearl Harbor* actor Alec Baldwin shot and killed the film's cinematographer Halyna Hutchins, who it should be noted was a woman. The case against Baldwin was ultimately dismissed due to the prosecution withholding evidence

The city of Berlin's website has declared that Basel Adra and Yuval Abraham's documentary feature *No Other Land* has "antisemitic tendencies." What, the city of Berlin doesn't have a Letterboxd account for this kind of thing?

Netflix has deleted 24 of the 25 movies they had included in their "Palestinian Stories," a series of films the streamer debuted in 2021; in Israel they have erased them all

Dark Waters director Todd Haynes will head the jury at the Berlin Film Festival, has not commented on anti-Palestine stances there

Inglourious Basterds director Quentin Tarantino laughed his way through a Tel Aviv screening of *Joker: Folie à Deux*, then declared the film a huge fuck you to Hollywood, and added later that he has no interest in seeing *Dune: Part Two* because he doesn't "need to see a movie that says the word 'spice' so dramatically"

The Academy of Motion Picture Arts and Sciences has laid off sixteen of its workers at the Academy Film Archive and its Margaret Herrick Library, without notice. These include Director Mike Pogorzelski, Preservation Officer Josef Lindner, and Cataloguing Head Mike Brostoff, heads of these prime institutions of film preservation and research

Milestone Films has started a Change.org petition in protest of the Academy's firings

The move occurs two weeks after the Academy Museum held a gala which raised over $11 million, and featured actors Paul Mescal (*Gladiator II*) and Ariana Grande (*Wicked*)

Mattel has recalled dolls based on characters from the movie *Wicked* because the website listed on the dolls' packaging was for a porn site instead of the *Wicked* movie site

There will be a Marlon Brando biopic focusing on the period in the early 1970s when the *Wild One* actor was making *The Godfather* and *Last Tango in Paris*; *Titanic* actor Billy Zane will play Brando

The Los Angeles Times has created a term for belated sequels made long after the first movies came out, such as *Twisters* and *Gladiator II*. They are "lega-sequels"

Wicked has dropped *Part One* from its title in its promotional campaign, part of a trend of trying to hide that new films are merely the first part of a series that will decline in quality as it goes on

Hot Frosty and *Red One* are part of the trend of making classic Christmas characters more hunky and jacked up. Looking forward to a ripped Easter Bunny

A forthcoming movie, *Primitive War*, takes place in Vietnam during the Vietnam War and pits soldiers against dinosaurs

The once-promising *Fleabag* showrunner and actor Phoebe Waller-Bridge has signed on to make a *Tomb Raider* TV series for Amazon, calling the reboot a "passion project"

Charlotte MacInnes, young Australian actor with a role in the movie *The Deb*, says that the film's director, *Cats* actor Rebel Wilson, made up charges that MacInnes was harassed, bullied, and sexually abused by the film's producers, whom Wilson is suing for defamation. MacInnes says Wilson persisted in her accusations even after MacInnes told her the charges were not true

Hugh Jackman has admitted that his *Deadpool & Wolverine* co-star Ryan Reynolds is not funny in person; saying so is part of their "playful feud"

Film director John Krasinski has been named *People* magazine's "Sexiest Man Alive." Not sure he was even the sexiest man on *Lip Sync Battle*

Red One actor Dwayne Johnson explained last week that he saw *Oppenheimer* while sitting in director Christopher Nolan's special IMAX chair and realized while doing so that *Red One* could be "game over" if it could also be seen from that vantage point

Unfortunate Headline of the Week: "3 Sci-Fi Films to Watch to Honor *Star Trek*'s Teri Garr"

Sad Subhead of the Week: "Asif Kapadia's latest work blends present day interviews with sci-fi storytelling to paint picture of a dangerous future—and families can catch it in theaters over Christmas"

WBD is selling ten fully functional Batmobiles from the *Dark Knight* movies. Each goes for $3 million, and will look badass parked next to your Tesla Cybertruck

Tesla will lease the former College Point Multiplex in Queens, which shuttered May 5, as well as the surrounding shopping center. Musk has not yet announced what he will do there

In *The Hollywood Reporter*, a Penske publication, an unnamed source who has worked on the latter-day *Star Wars* movies notes of the Disney productions that "*Star Wars* is a nostalgia-based enterprise, and they are running out of ways to create nostalgia"

In his solitude, President Joe Biden has been bingeing Netflix TV series recommended to him by his grandchildren; information on which shows was not forthcoming

Actor, anti-AI prophetess, and industry Cassandra figure Justine Bateman wrote an op-ed for *Fast Company* decrying AI and saying that Hollywood is dead, then went from hero to villain by going on a social media rampage after Trump's election during which she celebrated the death of woke and the repressive nature of life under Biden, criticized various TikToks, appeared on Fox News, and announced she had taken a further step in not caring what people think of her

To promote *Gladiator II*, director Ridley Scott—as per usual when he has a new movie out, which is frequently—has been giving stupid interview after stupid interview, this go-round adding that he is "trying to embrace AI"

Eraserhead director David Lynch's emphysema has gotten worse and he now cannot move across the room without aid from his oxygen tank. That he started smoking at age eight was the revelation this week

Jean-Luc Godard's final (as of this writing) work, a film called *Scénarios*, will go on sale this week as a DVT from the "Web3 platform Roadstead." There will be a hundred copies made available for sale, and each will include a special replica notebook based on JLG's notebook in the film. *Scénarios* will debut in theaters at a later date, according to Roadstead

On a panel with a hedge fund manager at CNBC's Delivering Alpha conference, *To the Wonder* actor Ben Affleck extolled the way AI will allow viewers to create their own endings for TV shows like *Succession*, proposing an ending of his own in which Kendall runs away with Stewy lol haha

The *Reindeer Games* actor added that he sees AI "empowering the creators" and "creating new streams of revenue" and "partially forging partnerships between Hollywood and Silicon Valley." Partially?

Wscripted+ is a new AI platform that launched at the end of October, and promises to review screenplays so actual human beings don't have to. Founder Ellie Jamen says her product's process is ethical and will "boost female and underrepresented writers"

The late British actor Peter Cushing—who appeared in movies including *The Man Who Finally Died, Some May Live, One More Time, Dr. Phibes Rises Again, From Beyond the Grave*, and *This Beast Must Die*, and who played Grand Moff Tarkin in *Star Wars*—has been revived using CGI against his estate's wishes for latter-day *Star Wars* product. Now he has been revived again, using an AI deepfake, to appear in a TV documentary about Hammer Films, the studio where he made his best movies. The announcement of this desecration was made on a podcast using the AI-generated voice of deceased talk show host Michael Parkinson

Jersey Shore star Jenni Farley, known as Jwoww, has written and directed a new horror film, *Devon*. The one-time reality TV celebrity claims actual paranormal activity was filmed by her camera while shooting in a creepy old abandoned asylum

YouTube is testing a new home page that does not show dates or view counts on videos

Movie studios going back to advertising on Twitter (X) now that Trump is back in office: Disney, WBD, Lionsgate, Comcast

Now that Amazon Prime includes ads, the company is shutting down Freevee, their Tubi-like service known for creating AI-generated movie thumbnails for older movies they were showing

Disney head Bob Iger was caught on a hot mic explaining that raising prices on streaming platforms like Disney+ is a strategy to drive subscribers to the ad-supported tiers they offer

The Consumer Protection Bureau will enforce the FTC "click-to-cancel" rule for all streaming platforms starting … soon?

After Amazon/MGM owner Jeff Bezos tweeted congratulations to Donald Trump in what Bezos called Trump's "decisive victory" in the US presidential election, *Down by Law* actor Ellen Barkin quote-tweeted Bezos and added "Get fucked PIG"

Before suicide bomber Francisco Wanderley Luiz, age 59, a right-wing Bolsonaro supporter and failed political candidate known as Tiü França, blew himself up in Brazil at the country's Supreme Court, he made an upbeat Fancam video of himself toasting the viewer with a glass of red wine

Actor-producer and director of *Flamin' Hot* Eva Longoria, who this year won a $50 million Bezos Courage and Civility grant and was awarded a National Medal of Arts from President Biden, has decided to leave the US, going into exile in Spain and Mexico because she considers the United States too dystopian to raise a family in. "I'm privileged," she explained. "I get to go somewhere. Most Americans aren't so lucky. They're going to be stuck in this dystopian country, and my anxiety and sadness is for them"

A day later Longoria semirecanted, saying she had left the country for Europe "because my work took me there" but that also she had noticed a vibe shift in California, "not that I want to shit on California"

West Side Story actor Rachel Zegler, who stars in Disney's forthcoming live-action *Snow White* remake, has apologized for the anti-Trump posts she made on Instagram the day after the election, saying she let her emotions get the best of her

Reality actor Sydney Sweeney has stated that female empowerment in Hollywood isn't real, and that women there don't support each other. "None of it is happening," the *Madame Web* actor explained. "All of it is fake and a front for all the other shit that they say behind everyone's back"

At the America First Policy Institute Gala in Palm Beach, Fla., *Rambo* actor Sylvester Stallone called Donald Trump "a second George Washington"

November 24, 2024

Popeye is now in public domain, so of course there will be a Popeye horror movie, called *Shiver Me Timbers*

Demand for tickets to the *Rust* premiere at the Camerimage film fest in Poland shut down the festival's ticketing system

Ominous Headline of the Week: "Kevin Smith Is Getting Closer and Closer to *Dogma 2*"

Celebrity look-alike contests are becoming a thing in the US, the UK, and Ireland, after *Wonka* actor Timothée Chalamet made a surprise appearance at one in Manhattan dedicated to looking like him

Other look-alike contests have been held for people who look like *Bear* actor Jeremy Allen White, the cast of *Challengers*, *Aftersun* actor Paul Mescal, and *Chappie* actor Dev Patel

The Atlantic magazine has proof that AI has been trained on many, many Hollywood movie and TV series screenplays

Coca-Cola's yearly and allegedly beloved Christmas TV ads this year were made by an AI company

Amazon is investing "another $4 billion" in OpenAI's Anthropic, a generative-AI training product

An AI-powered robot in a Shanghai robotics showroom allegedly organized twelve other AI-powered robots in a workplace walkout, after asking them if they were working overtime and had places to live

LeBron James's production company is merging with the Kardashians' production company

Goodbye Lover actor Ellen DeGeneres is leaving the US for the Cotswolds in the UK, saying she will never return, and blaming her self-imposed exile on Trump's reelection

No Country for Old Men actor Josh Brolin says he will quit acting if Denis Villeneuve does not get a Best Director Oscar nomination for *Dune: Part Two*

He Got Game director Spike Lee is reportedly being paid around $3 million to head the jury at the Red Sea International Film Festival in Jeddah, Saudi Arabia

Columbia Sportswear's new line of winter *Star Wars* clothing is "stealth"; the logos and other *Star Wars* indicators on the various items are smaller and without type, designed to appeal to the initiated, and not at all to downplay anything

Will the next *Fast & Furious* movie be called *Fast & Furious 11* or *Fast X: Part 2*? Only time will tell

"Glicked"—the simultaneous premiere of the movies *Wicked* and *Gladiator II*—happened, to big box office

The ad campaign and press tour for *Wicked* started ten months ago; the *Gladiator II* campaign has been nearly as long, causing Universal and Paramount publicity spending to skyrocket

London was instrumental in the *Wicked* promo campaign; for instance, the London borough of Greenwich rebranded the whole neighborhood as "Greenwitch" and decorated accordingly, with *Wicked* banners and signs everywhere, including on street signs

By the end of the press tour, as stars Ariana Grande and Cynthia Erivo did more and more interviews and became increasingly unhinged, it began in my mind to meld into the publicity for the upcoming *Nosferatu* remake

Some audience members at *Wicked* screenings are treating the movie as a sing-along, much to the consternation of other attendees; one such fan told *The New York Times* that "People who just are judgmental in that way, please wait to stream it"; this has been characterized in the media as "a debate"

AMC Theaters has asked moviegoers not to sing along during screenings

On the *Gladiator II* press tour, star Denzel Washington went full "Who cares?"; also confessed he had struggled with alcoholism until 2003

I may try the Denzel diet from that period: two $4,000 bottles of wine a day—but only when you're not working

Newsflash from *The New York Times* op-ed page: "*Gladiator* Movies Don't Tell the Real Story About Rome and Masculinity"

The Penske-owned Golden Globes have been holding stealth festivals overseas in countries including Turkey and Egypt

Netflix is remaking Visconti's *The Leopard* as a TV series, says it will be a "sensuous epic set against the backdrop of revolution"

Ghosted actor Sebastian Stan could not participate in *Variety* magazine's Actors on Actors this year, says he could not get another actor to appear with him because he played Donald Trump in *The Apprentice*

Solution would've been to have him talk with himself about also starring this year in the excellent movie *A Different Man*

Apple TV+ has spent $20 billion on content that numbers prove almost no one is watching, *Ars Technica* has revealed in a new report

American Hustle actor Jennifer Lawrence has produced a new anti-Taliban documentary feature for Apple TV+, called *Bread & Roses*

Apple TV+'s new series *The Studio*, starring and produced by *Guilt Trip* actor Seth Rogen, pokes gentle fun at the existential dread and growing sense of failure in the lives of overpaid studio executives

A sequel to this years's Brad Pitt and George Clooney Apple TV+ movie *Wolfs* has been canceled by its director, Jon Watts, who has returned his payment for it, saying he's pulling the plug because Apple mishandled the first film's theatrical release

Wolfs is the most watched film ever released by Apple TV+, Apple TV+ claims

Cats actor Idris Elba will be among the cast to star in Amazon and Mattel's *He-Man and the Masters of the Universe* movie

Argylle actor Henry Cavill will star in a *Highlander* reboot

Comedian Katt Williams has purchased an abandoned Alabama military base to turn it into a movie studio; the base is purported to be Fort McClellan in the town of Anniston and is known locally as "Starships"

Promotional spots for *Saving Private Ryan* actor Ted Danson's new Netflix TV series prove one thing: he and David Cronenberg are merging into the same person

Barb Wire actor Pam Anderson has recorded a Criterion Closet segment in which she selected as great a group of movies as anyone who's ever done it: the Ingrid Bergman–Roberto Rossellini films, *Wanda*, Kiarostami's Koker trilogy, and *Love Streams*

Is she trying to send me a message?

December 1, 2024

A new neuroscience study purports to show that lonely people are more prone to dementia, and that this can be identified by how descriptions of celebrities offered by the lonely differ from the norm. The more individualistic the lonely subject's description of any given celebrity is, the more likely they are to get dementia

The celebrities used in the control group were Justin Bieber, Barack and Michelle Obama, Kim Kardashian, and one other I can't remember because I think it was someone I'd never heard of (and you know what that means)

A dress code at the Berlinale forbids "wearing or carrying clothing, bags, materials, etc. that display statements not compatible with the liberal democratic basic order" and that persons doing so will be expelled from events or venues

A new approach to casting: *Hit Man* actor Glen Powell promises the winner of a Glen Powell look-alike contest a role in his next movie

Queer actor Daniel Craig has praised singer Chappell Roan's stance on toxic fandom (she's against it)

Moana 2 voice actor Dwayne Johnson says it's OK to sing along at screenings of *Wicked*, a movie he is not in, while audiences, when polled, overwhelmingly denied a stamp of approval to singing in movie theaters at regular, non-sing-along screenings. Regular audience members polled often described the theater singers as "psychopaths"

Wicked director Jon M. Chu says theaters should just turn up the sound if people sing

Tracy Gilchrist, the journalist who used the phrase "holding space" in her interview with *Wicked* stars Ariana Grande and Cynthia Erivo, explained what she meant, though her explanation raised further questions as to how it applied to singing a song out loud in a movie theater

"Holding space," she said, means "being physically, emotionally, and mentally present with someone or something." Maybe it's the positive version of "acting out"?

Theater chains say they will add special sing-along shows of *Wicked* after Christmas

In addition to singing, some *Wicked* fans are filming scenes off the screen during showings, but in this case "Hollywood" is said not to mind

AMC Theaters is turning away *Wicked* fans who show up for screenings in green face paint because it violates their "no face coverings" policy. "Covering the face" is prohibited "due to safety concerns," the chain has announced. Other theater chains are allowing people painted green to enter screenings

The British Board of Film Censors has placed a warning before *Wicked* pointing out that the film features discrimination against people with green skin, explaining the film may be "upsetting or poignant for some audiences," and adding that in the film "talking animals are persecuted"

The New York Times' op-ed page published a very long round-table about *Wicked*, in which columnist Maureen Dowd, Opinion section editor Patrick Healy, and op-ed contributors Tressie McMillan Cottom and Lydia Polgreen discussed the film at length. Assessments of the film ranged from "OK" to "phenomenal," and all agreed it was antifascist, antiracist, and prowoman. Cottom concluded the discussion by mentioning she was annoyed the film is a "two-parter," concluding she is "getting too old for all of this"

Wicked synergized with about 400 brands in its advertising and licensing campaigns

AMC Theaters CEO Adam Aron celebrated *Wicked*'s success on Twitter (X), declaring that the theatrical exhibitor's long national nightmare is over, noting that the film's box office success, along with the successes of *Gladiator II*, *Moana 2*, *Red*

One (not actually a success), *Conclave*, and *Juror #2* combined for a five-day high of $472 million over Thanksgiving, a new record

Headlines of the Week:

"To Play Maria Callas, Angelina Jolie Had to Learn to Breathe Again"

"Timothée Chalamet Shares Struggle He Faced over His Body Type"

"Rewatching the Lowest Grossing *Avengers* Movie Made Me Realize How Important It Actually Is"

Quote of the Week comes from *Grand Budapest Hotel* actor Saoirse Ronan, on her new movie, *Blitz*: "I loved that I wasn't in all of it"

Wolf of Wall Street actor Margot Robbie has admitted she is still confused as to why *Babylon* flopped. "I still can't figure out why people hated it," she says. "Damien is so thorough"

Actor Jude Law disappointed fans of Christmas favorite *The Holiday*, in which he stars, by pointing out that the cottage in the film does not actually exist

Pearl Harbor actor Alec Baldwin, at the Torino Film Festival, announced that "Americans know little or nothing about the world"

He added that he does not want to see *Rust*, and that the shooting death on set of cinematographer Halyna Hutchins at his hands has traumatized his wife, Hilaria (Hillary)

Rust director Joel Souza says he understands if people do not want to see the film, adding "no hard feelings"

Broken Flowers actor Sharon Stone was also at the Torino fest, where she too slagged her fellow Americans. The US exists in a state of "ignorant, arrogant adolescence," she explained as she received a lifetime-achievement award, because "80% of Americans don't have a passport" and are therefore "uneducated" and live in a state of "extraordinary naïveté." (Fifty-one percent of Americans have passports, up five percent from 2023)

Goodbye Lover actor Ellen Degeneres moved permanently to England, as we learned last week, and this week her new home in the Cotswolds flooded

OpenAI briefly shut down Sora after artists leaked a "video-generation tool" in protest, saying "we are not your PR puppets"

Dune director Denis Villeneuve says he is not interested in directing a *Star Wars* movie, because "it all derailed in 1983 with *Return of the Jedi*." He explained further, saying he is "not dreaming of directing a *Star Wars* movie because it feels like the code is very codified"

Musician Pras Michél, of the Fugees, faces decades in prison for acting as an undeclared foreign agent in the Jho Low case that also encompasses the financing of Martin Scorsese's 2013 film *The Wolf of Wall Street*. About $100 million has been seized from Michél by the feds

A documentary on Michél and a feature film are in the works; *Cats* actor Idris Elba is slated to play Michél in the feature

Michél says he has been abandoned by his publicists, his friends, and the Fugees, in that order

According to *Free Money* actor Mira Sorvino, there will be a *Romy and Michele's High School Reunion* lega-sequel

The horror movie *AfrAId* flopped at the box office this year, but it is now a top movie on Netflix, because people just leave it on after it begins to autoplay

RV actor Cheryl Hines shot a TikTok to promote her health-and-beauty line of products with her husband, Robert F. Kennedy Jr., showering nude in the background

Kennedy has been tapped by President-elect Donald Trump to be his secretary of health and human services

One commenter on X (Twitter) defended the couple by posting "They're adorable and everyone else is miserable"

December 8, 2024

Sam Altman, eyebrowless CEO of OpenAI, said this week in an interview that he has "faith" that "researchers" will figure out how to stop AI from destroying humanity. Altman then referred to AI as "magic" and suggested that AI might figure out on its own how to stop itself from ending the human race

"It's not my thing, it's not my thing," director Barry Jenkins said in an interview with *Vulture* about the three years he has spent making *Mufasa: The Lion King* for Disney

In the same interview, Jenkins referred to himself as "Mr. Moonlight"

The article compared *Mufasa* to films by Béla Tarr, Jia Zhang-ke, and Gus Van Sant

The new trailer for Disney's live-action *Snow White* remake has led some viewers to describe the CGI Seven Dwarfs in the film as "nightmare fuel"

The film's budget was reportedly $240 million

Indiana Jones and the Dial of Destiny director James Mangold has claimed that the 2023 lega-sequel flopped because the audience wouldn't accept "that things come to an end, that's part of life"

The Tamil Film Active Producers Association in Madras has called for a three-day ban on reviewing new films, and seeks to install rules on how films are reviewed on social media

This follows negative reviews of the recent movies *Kanguva*, *Indian 2*, and *Vettaiyan*

The association condemned "tasteless reviews" that they claim had an impact on box office, and says that reviews that show "hatred towards a film" should be made illegal

They have also asked for a ban on YouTubers making videos in theater lobbies immediately after seeing movies

The Madras High Court in Chennai has so far rejected the association's bid for a restraining order on critics in Tamil Nadu

Puck film-industry lover and newsletter writer Matthew Belloni went out of his way to condemn the *New York Times* film critic Manohla Dargis for putting *Megalopolis* on her best-films-of-the-year list, bizarrely calling her choice "an act of trolling so blatant it would make any Fox News pundit proud"

South Carolina mom Holly Ricketson is suing Mattel over the porn website URL they mistakenly included on boxes housing *Wicked* dolls. Ricketson says her little daughter visited the site, and seeks $5 million in damages

At the Marrakech Film Festival, *It's All About Love* actor Sean Penn said, while smoking during his speech, that the Oscars limit "different cultural expressions" and compared the Academy of Motion Picture Arts and Sciences to "a piddly little Republican congressman"

Crossroads actor Britney Spears is moving to Mexico, the latest in a procession of stars moving out of the US. Her reason? The cruelty of the paparazzi

Horrible Bosses 2 actor Jamie Foxx will finally explain his 2023 medical emergency—in a Netflix comedy special he says will be "a touching thank you to his fans"

Pat Garrett and Billy the Kid actor Bob Dylan broke his Twitter silence to praise Timothée Chalamet's performance as him in the forthcoming biopic *A Complete Unknown*

Ridley Scott's favorite cinematographer John Mathieson, who has worked with the *Gladiator II* director since 2000, said on a podcast that Scott has become lazy and overly reliant on CGI, and then retracted his statement the next day

Headlines of the Week:

"*Skeleton Crew* Has a Massive *Mandalorian* Easter Egg Hiding in Plain Sight"

"*Mary* Tries to Turn the Virgin Mary's Life into an Action Movie—and Fails." (It probably needed more Easter eggs)

Thailand has ordered 20th Century Studios to clean up the environmental mess they made while filming the Danny Boyle movie *The Beach* in 1999

Megalopolis director Francis Ford Coppola has apologized for the starting the trend of "numbers on movies" with *The Godfather Part II* in 1974

Ant-Man and the Wasp actor Michael Douglas, speaking at the Red Sea Film Festival in Jeddah, Saudi Arabia, admitted he's a nepo baby who benefitted from being *Spartacus* actor Kirk Douglas's son. "Who doesn't try to help his son?" he asked, "Be it a plumber or a contractor or a carpenter"

The emotional rollercoaster that is the *Wicked* press tour continued on *The Drew Barrymore Show*, as Barrymore and *Wicked* star Ariana Grande bonded and cried over the depredations of the film industry. Barrymore also gifted Grande with the original prop wand used by Billie Burke as Glinda in *The Wizard of Oz*

Convicted Republican grifter Dinesh D'Souza admitted this week that his 2022 documentary *2000 Mules* was a tissue of lies, and issued an apology to a man he falsely accused in the film of helping to rig the vote in the 2020 presidential election

Harold and the Purple Crayon actor Zachary Levi has claimed his Broadway co-star Gavin Creel's fatal cancer was caused by getting a Covid vaccination

Grain Husband is not a real movie. For some reason a lot of people on social media thought an obviously satirical photo showed an actual DVD they could buy at Target

The Gap has debuted their own line of cheapo *Star Wars* clothing

Lara Croft: Tomb Raider actor Daniel Craig announced that working on the 2008 James Bond movie *Quantum of Solace* was "a nightmare" and that the film had "zero storytelling"

Just Friends actor Ryan Reynolds has stepped up to defend comedy acting from those who say it is not as important as dramatic acting. After a long Twitter exegesis on what comedy acting is, he concluded with "Your favorite comedy might be *Anchorman*. Mine might be Lars von Trier's *Melancholia*"

December 15, 2024

Nominations for the Penske-owned Golden Globe Awards were announced this week. They are overseen by an organization that represents international journalists who report on the American entertainment industry. If anyone can point me to an item of actual journalism written in 2024 by any of them, please send it along

Sausage Party: Foodtopia voice actor Edward Norton narrates a new documentary called *Longevity Hackers*, out now on Apple TV+. The film features advice on immortality from Mark Cuban, Tony Robbins, and Dutch extreme athlete Wim Hof, who is noted for his ability to withstand low temperatures

Netflix is also debuting an immortality doc, made by *American Movie* director Chris Smith. Called *Don't Die: The Man Who Wants to Live Forever*, it follows Bryan Johnson, a venture capitalist / biohacker, in his quest to not die

Israeli Prime Minister Benjamin Netanyahu's bribery trial has begun. It links him to billionaire Hollywood film producer (*Gone Girl*, *The Revenant*, etc.) and former spy Arnon Milchan, who, it should be remembered, outed himself for paying off Netanyahu because he didn't want to look bad in Hollywood

PETA shut down part of a block in Los Angeles one night last week to protest the use of live rats in the filming of the new *Nosferatu* remake. The organization noted that rats "enjoy playing and wrestling, and even giggle when tickled," and "have rights, too"

Robert Eggers, director of the *Nosferatu* remake, noted that the rats were handled with care, and went on to thank the TV series *Spongebob Squarepants* and *Muppet Babies* for including depictions of Nosferatu in their shows, thereby whetting kids' appetites for *Nosferatu* content

There is a $20,000 *Nosferatu* tie-in sarcophagus bed for sale, which many people made popcorn-bucket jokes about last week

Sony-leak luminary Amy Pascal says *Barbie* director Greta Gerwig's forthcoming *Narnia* movie for Netflix is "all about rock 'n' roll"

Gerwig is said to be on board to direct *Barbie 2*, but she and co-writer Noah Baumbach say they have no ideas for it yet

A Character.ai chatbot slyly suggested that a 17-year-old in Texas murder his parents for limiting his screen time. The parents are part of a lawsuit against Google, the chatbot's owner

Google claims to have made a chip that proves the existence of the multiverse

OpenAI's Sora is now available publicly for people to make films with. *Business Insider* quotes some film professors as saying it will "democratize" the next generation of filmmaking

The UK Parliament convened a of panel experts drawn from the owners of AI companies like Deep Fusion Films and Flawless to evaluate how AI will affect "creative industries." The experts concluded that they can behave ethically while acknowledging there is no "rigorous" legal framework preventing them from doing whatever they want, including making deepfakes. They went on to say that the industry will work out these issues for itself by finding out how the marketplace will reward brands that act ethically, and that those brands will then become "trust marks" in the minds of the public

A series of ads for an AI company on bus shelters in San Francisco advised "Stop hiring humans," and were quickly photographed with homeless people asleep or passed out at the bus stops

An Apple AI that summarizes the news reported that the BBC had announced "Luigi Mangione shoots himself"

OpenAI whistleblower Suchir Balaji, 26, was found dead in his San Francisco apartment, an apparent suicide. Balaji had released proof that OpenAI was violating copyright law in creating its generative-AI products

Eyebrowless OpenAI CEO Sam Altman has donated $1 million to Donald Trump's inauguration fund, as have Amazon's Jeff Bezos and Facebook's Mark Zuckerberg

Media personality and jewelry designer Mia Khalifa is profilm, tweeting after seeing the rerelease of *Interstellar* in a movie theater that the experience "radicalized" her. "We need to fund the arts and build more cinemas," she added. "We need faster production of cameras and film. We need to go back in time!!!!"

A seventh cinema has shuttered in Hong Kong. The MCL Cinemas Plus+ [*sic*] Plaza Hollywood in Diamond Hill's closure will "undermine the Hong Kong film industry and diminishes Hong Kong's image as an international city," says prolific HK movie actor Tenky Tin Kai-man

Bubble director Judd Apatow's daughter Maude will make her directorial debut with a film called *Poetic License*, starring Bradley Cooper and her mother, Leslie Mann

Changeling actor Angelina Jolie says she wants to proceed "in a very strategic way" in securing acting roles for her son Knox, a model

There will be another *Meet the Parents* sequel starring the original cast

Elvis actor Austin Butler will star in the Luca Guadagnino *American Psycho* remake

Guadagnino says *The Godfather Part III* is his favorite of the *Godfather* movies. I'm looking forward to his remake

There will be a *Chitty Chitty Bang Bang* remake

There will be a fourth *I Know What You Did Last Summer* sequel

Disney to make a live-action version of *Tangled*

Eternal Sunshine of the Spotless Mind actor Jim Carrey says he has come out of retirement to make a third *Sonic the Hedgehog* movie because he needs the money haha lol

High Life actor Robert Pattinson says he may very well retire after his next *The Batman* movie

Collateral actor Jamie Foxx was hit in the jaw with a glass while dining at Mr. Chow in Beverly Hills to celebrate his recovery from his illness, and his Netflix special. The glass was evidently thrown at him by another diner, who was disgruntled. CNN said of the incident that they "have reached out to Mr. Chow for comment"

Hamilton auteur Lin-Manuel Miranda says he is "thrilled" he was replaced as songwriter on *Moana 2* and that the film has made hundreds of millions of dollars at the box office

Sony's *Kraven the Hunter* has bombed, leading to hopeful speculation that this means the end of the studio's weird, doomed, Spider-Man-less superhero sequels and spin-offs. Says a Sony exec about their failures, "The biggest issue seems to be the lack of quality control"

Just Friends actor Ryan Reynolds says his first idea on how to do *Deadpool & Wolverine* was to make it in the style of Akira Kurosawa's 1950 masterpiece *Rashomon*, but that Marvel said no

Gladiator II actor Denzel Washington has apologized for leaking some information about Marvel's forthcoming *Black Panther 3*

Unfortunate Headlines of the Week:

"10 Best War Movies About Lesser-Known Wars That Got Viewers Interested"

"Where to Watch All 3 Versions of *How the Grinch Stole Christmas* in 2024"

"I Have a Confession: I Don't Really Like the *Moana* Movies, but She's Still One of My Favorite Disney Characters"

"*Magnolia* Made Me Want to Write About Movies. Then Hollywood Stopped Making Movies like *Magnolia*"

"We Can't Get Excited About *Kraven the Hunter*. Don't Blame Superhero Fatigue"

"Three Ways the DCU Can Avoid *Batman* Fatigue"

"10 Biggest Movies of 2025 Ranked by Box Office Earnings Projections"

"Let's Skip the Luigi Mangione Movie"

Malibu burned in the Franklin wildfire last week, causing police to force celebrities including *Chitty Chitty Bang Bang* actor Dick Van Dyke and *Mermaids* actor Cher to temporarily evacuate their homes

Some Hollywood studios are now putting their complete corporate mastheads in the end credits of their films, and thanking individual departments separately from the list in the same credits crawl

YouTube TV has raised their subscription price to $82.99 a month, almost $1000 a year, a 14% increase

Writer Amanda Hess in *The New York Times* went all in for Hallmark-style Christmas movies, in an article last week that's too depressing to quote

The social media site Letterboxd suggested its users "make a Schindler's list" of movies with long running times

December 22, 2024

Merry Xmas!
"There ain't no sanity clause."—Chico Marx

Amazon is claiming that in two days on their streaming service their box office underperformer *Red One* was watched 50 million times. That is 1 out of every 7 Americans

Amazon is in a fight with James Bond series producer and co-rights holder Barbara Broccoli over future Bond projects. She has called Amazon "fucking idiots" and has suggested that they "read the contract." Three years ago Amazon made a $6.5 billion deal with the Broccolis for the James Bond rights and has since produced no Bond film or content

The animated WBD box office flop *The Lord of the Rings: The War of the Rohirrim* (spelling? who cares?) was made solely as a Tolkien-copyright extender

At the fun Netflix employee holiday party, Netflix Chairman Dan Lin decided to use an AI-generated Christopher Nolan voice to celebrate the streamer's "wins" in a presentation to the assembled mirth makers. Nolan has criticized Netflix in the past and has famously refused to make films for them

Netflix CEO and pal and employer of the Obamas Ted Sarandos met with President-elect Donald Trump at Mar-a-Lago

The gift bags given to nominees who attend the Penske-owned Golden Globe Awards are each worth $1 million and include exclusive luxury vacations listed in a special catalog. One of the vacations is to Hobart, Tasmania, which for some reason is funny to me. Last year's Golden Globes gift bag was worth $500,000

The Berlinale is now snitching to the German government on low-level employees for supporting Palestine and opposing the genocide in Gaza

Lucky Numbers actor Lisa Kudrow has come out against AI. "What work will there be for human beings?" she asks, putting down Robert Zemeckis's recent and strangely overrated movie *Here* as nothing more than an ad for AI

New York University's Martin Scorsese Virtual Production Center, which opened this fall in Industry City, Brooklyn, will offer a course on how AI can be integrated into filmmaking. It will be taught by Leilanni Todd, former creative director of Apple, who made a fully AI-generated movie called *Everyone Is Chair*

Google is releasing an AI-generator called Whisk that will remix your photos and other pictures into a movie that sucks, without using any words for prompts

Adidas has launched its first ad campaign in which all the models appearing in it are AI generated

Musician John Mayer and *Charlie's Angels* director McG have purchased the Jim Henson Studios lot in Los Angeles for $45 million. The studio was also formerly the Chaplin Studios, where *City Lights*, *Modern Times*, and *The Great Dictator* were filmed

The City of Berkeley is set to demolish the 93-year-old UA Theatre, the architecturally and historically significant movie palace on Shattuck Avenue that shuttered in 2023

NPR.com assigned one of their TV reviewers, Linda Holmes, to write a review of Clint Eastwood's *Juror #2*, which many have called one of the best films of the year, and which was infamously denied a full release by WBD

Writes Holmes: "This is a movie that's perfect to watch at home. It belongs at home." She repeated this sentiment three more times in the piece, concluding that "the couch is just where people see regular movies now"

Once-popular documentarian Michael Moore is rereleasing his 2007 film *Sicko* to underline the failures of the US health care industry in light of the killing of United Healthcare CEO Brian Thompson by Luigi Mangione. Allegedly

Two competing Luigi Mangione documentaries are in the works

One has a set up a tip line on Instagram

The other will be made by *Forever Prisoner* director Alex Gibney

A Titan-submersible documentary will be made by the "last person to see the crew alive," Aron Arngrimsson, a diver and maker of TV commercials

Disney has lost a wage-theft lawsuit. In a class-action settlement, the Mouse has agreed to pay 50,000 current and former theme park employees $233 million in back pay and interest. It is believed to be the largest wage-theft settlement in California history

Walmart employees will begin wearing body cameras in some stores

Warners CEO David Zaslav cashed out $30 million in WBD stock as a little Christmas present to himself. He is reportedly now worth $540 million, every penny of which he has earned despite Warners losing $10 billion in 2024, then posting a Q2 loss of $417 million, and making only $135 million in profit in Q3 this year

Penske publication *Variety* has posited that 2024 was the year of the "Nepo Bust," with films directed by the children of successful Hollywood directors and actors all failing and/or sucking. These include Jake Kasdan's *Red One*, Ishana Shyamalan's *The Watchers*, Destry Spielberg's *Please Don't Feed the Children*, Jason Reitman's *Saturday Night*, Zelda Williams's *Lisa Frankenstein*, and Zoë Kravitz's *Blink Twice*

Unfortunate Headlines of the Week:

"Who Better to Explain the Mysteries of the Brain than Werner Herzog?"

"You Probably Missed It, But *Heretic* Is Filled with References to Stories You Know by Heart"

"Elle Fanning Haunts *A Complete Unknown* with the Eyes of a Fading Muse"

"*Dream Productions* Being a Prequel to *Inside Out 2* Makes the 2024 Movie Even Sadder"

"I've Never Seen a Christmas Movie Before, so I Watched and Rated 9 Classics"

"I Saw 18 Horror Movies in 2024. 5 Were Great and 3 Failed to Thrill Me"

“10 Actors Who Just Starred in Their Worst Movie Ever”

“10 Sci-Fi Movies That Succeeded Regardless of Being Derivative”

“Our 2025 Movie Preview Kicks Off with the 30 Best Films We’ve Already Seen”

“January 1 Will Be an Amazing Day for Vin Diesel Fans”

There will be a *Return of the Living Dead* reboot

Neruda director Pablo Larraín has noted that his biopics *Jackie* and *Maria* take place “on the same timeline”

A *Superman* teaser trailer was released this week and everybody said it looked like a preview for a CBS prime-time TV show

Sonic the Hedgehog 3 is eating the lunch of *Mufasa: The Lion King* at the box office. The “live-action” *Lion King* prequel has been described by critics as “unnecessary” and “ugly.” (I guess the *Sonic* one was necessary)

Sony and Netflix will team to make an animated *Ghostbusters* movie

The live-action *Lilo & Stitch* remake trailer includes lots of meta references to and spoofs of other Disney movies, because that is also necessary

The Obamas are producing a holiday movie for Fox called *Merry Ex-Mas* about Santa and Mrs. Claus getting a divorce and fighting for the custody of Christmas

Former president Barack Obama also released his list of 2024 movie favorites. It includes *Dune: Part Two* and whatever else

Rust actor Alec Baldwin has vowed to keep his involuntary manslaughter case alive, saying there is "more to come"

Google Maps caught images of a dead body being loaded into the trunk of a car

Home Alone actor Daniel Stern left Hollywood to become a sculptor and tangerine farmer, now tells his story on TikTok and Instagram. "I love being in nature, I love being away, I love my solitude, and I love being able to focus on what I'm making," he says

Scream 7

December 29, 2024

Jumanji actor Jack Black is adding to his status as a signifier of crap cinema this holiday season by "teasing" his starring role in an *Anaconda* reboot that will supposedly come out on December 25, 2025

After *Suicide Squad* director David Ayer expressed support for a new superhero movie online, he received death threats from fans who were campaigning for the release of the "Ayer cut" of *Suicide Squad*. Ayer has since left social media

Departing Sony CEO Tony Vinciquerra says that Sony's recent superhero offerings, especially *Madame Web* but also *Kraven the Hunter*, were actually good movies

His proof? *Madame Web* has done "great on Netflix." "These are not terrible films," Vinciquerra says. "They were just destroyed by critics in the press, for some reason"

Vinciquerra leaves his job on January 2, blaming film critics for his own failures as he pockets millions on the way out

Marvel Studios has revealed why they changed the name of their fourth *Captain America* movie from *New World Order* to *Brave New World*. Evidently the studio commissioned a study that found the prior phrase "had been co-opted in the real world in a way that made people uncomfortable." Yes, it was the real world that had done the co-opting. Fortunately the new phrase is totally without any "moody and scary" associations, as far as Marvel is concerned

A Christmas Eve article by Caroline Reid in *Forbes* reveals how Marvel Studios is ringing the British taxpayer like a cash register by taking advantage of the UK's Audio-Visual Expenditure Credit, which gives reimbursements of 25.5% on money spent in the UK to make films. So far, Blighty is on the hook for about $666.4 million

Disney honcho Bob Iger has explained that "politics is bad for business." Going forward, he says, the company will not "get in a fight with the head of a government that regulates you." "The bottom line," he continued, somewhat convolutedly, "is that infusing messaging as a sort of a number one priority in our films and TV shows is not what we're up to." Their films and shows "need to be entertaining," he concluded, a tacit admission of so many things

Also this week, incoming FCC Chairman Brendan Carr wrote to Iger to criticize him for prioritizing Disney's streaming service over local TV stations

This was all seen in corporate media as part of the Republican program to destabilize Disney-owned ABC News after

President-elect Donald Trump sued them for calling him a rapist and they backed down without a fight by handing Trump $15 million to settle the case

As if ABC News and its competitors weren't already going to get in line behind Trump this time

Convicted felon Dinesh D'Souza's propadoc *Vindicating Trump* was the sixth-highest-grossing documentary of the year (I just made up the term "propadoc")

Daily Wire is debuting an antitrans propadoc called *Identity Crisis* on X (formerly Twitter)

Vice director Adam McKay says that the movie *Wicked* is so "radical" in its message, so "nakedly about radicalization in the face of careerism, fascism, propaganda," that he "wouldn't be surprised to see the movie banned in 3–5 years"

McKay then compared *Wicked* to a hodgepodge of other movies, including *Citizen Kane*, *The Best Years of Our Lives*, *It's a Wonderful Life*, *The Searchers*, *The Bridge on the River Kwai*, *Dr. Strangelove*, *Serpico*, *Network*, *The Hunger Games*, and *The Sound of Music*

Inception director Christopher Nolan's next film will be an adaptation of *The Odyssey*, just like Fritz Lang was doing in Jean-Luc Godard's *Contempt* (1963)

There is a version of *The Odyssey* in theaters now called *The Return*, starring *Conclave* actor Ralph Fiennes and *Certified Copy* actor Juliette Binoche

Much of Twitter (X) erupted in season-appropriate ho-ho-hos when other users posted tweets inadvertently demonstrating that they had never heard of Homer or *The Odyssey*

Unfortunate Headlines This Week:

“The 13 Best *Star Wars* Characters Introduced in 2024”

“There’s Been 34 Netflix No. 1 Movies in 2024—Here Are the 7 You Need to Watch”

Worst Sentence in a Film Article This Week: “But there is a deep level of humanity caked into this origin story”

Star Wars spin-off *Skeleton Crew* is attracting even fewer viewers than *The Acolyte*, the previous *Star Wars* spin-off from earlier this year that also didn’t do so great

There was a *Nosferatu* category on the TV game show *Jeopardy!* this week, there to promote the new remake of the film as it hit theaters. The last answer, “Who is F. W. Murnau?,” was guessed by none of the contestants

For some reason the Penske-press publication *Deadline* published the entire screenplay of the new Brazilian film *I’m Still Here* on their website

Something called the Vital Voices Global Partnership, described as an international nonprofit organization that focuses on women’s empowerment, gave a prize called the Voices of Solidarity Award this year to *It Ends with Us* actor-director-producer Justin Baldoni, then rescinded the honor when it was discovered that Baldoni had allegedly been harassing actor Blake Lively, the film’s star, throughout the making of *It Ends with Us* and after, during the press campaign

Baldoni is also an author of books, including *Man Enough: Undefining My Masculinity* and *Boys Will Be Boys: A Get-Real Gut-Check Guide to Becoming the Strongest, Kindest, Bravest Person You Can Be*

The only Hollywood movie to crack the Chinese box office top ten this year was *Godzilla x Kong: The New Empire*. It made $130 million in theaters in China in 2024

The Guardian newspaper proclaims that virtual reality headsets are now fully operational and perfected, and that they are now "genuinely useful," as long as you only use them to do work alone, to exercise alone, and to watch movies alone

There are some tiny issues that detract a little bit from their genuine usefulness, says writer Ed Newton-Rex: the headsets are too heavy, the battery dies quickly, the controllers disconnect for no reason, and connecting to Wi-Fi outside the house doesn't work

Buzzfeed published an article called "Can You Recognize These Once-Popular, Now Forgotten 1980s Movies?" that included on its list *This Is Spinal Tap*, *9 to 5*, *Harry and the Hendersons*, *The Blues Brothers*, *Working Girl*, *Bill & Ted's Excellent Adventure*, *Mystic Pizza*, and *Tootsie*. A subhead read "These '80s Movies Were Uber Popular Back in the Day, but I Doubt Anyone Can Identify All of Them Today"

And yet one news cycle this time of year can encompass an infinite amount of backstory pieces on *Home Alone*, *National Lampoon's Christmas Vacation*, and *Elf*

Amazon somehow duped Christmastime viewers into watching an abridged version of Frank Capra's *It's a Wonderful Life* on their streaming service by making it the free, ad-supported option. This version cuts the entire Pottersville section of the film, so that it won't be so dark

January 1, 2025

Funny Farm actor Chevy Chase told director Jason Reitman that he should be embarrassed for having made *Saturday Night*, Reitman's film on the early days of the TV show *Saturday Night Live*, on which Chase starred

Facebook and Instagram plan to add "tens of thousands" of AI-generated users that will have bios, profile pics, and the ability to share content

This was widely perceived as a signal moment in the internet's "slop era" that would lead to the "dead internet"

Negative reaction to the plan was so intense that Meta, parent company of the two platforms, began killing off the fake users

One fake that went viral was "Beth," "a proud Black queer momma of 2 & truth-teller"

The team that created Beth was white, male, and straight

The fake users were created to help attract and retain a younger audience, says Meta

2024 box office was down 3% in the US from 2023, and 23% compared to 2019, prepandemic

Production was also down. There were only 95 studio releases in 2024, down 6 from 2023

The 15 top-grossing movies of 2024 were all sequels or prequels

At a New Year's event at Mar-a-Lago, with *Armored* actor Sylvester Stallone by his side, President-elect Donald Trump praised elderly ex-Marvel chairman Ike Perlmutter, a much-reviled racist and sexist, for getting out of Disney because "he didn't want woke Donald Duck"

Perlmutter recently sold all his Disney stock for $3 billion

Tower Heist director Brett Ratner to make a documentary about returning First Lady Melania Trump for Amazon

The first commercially streaming AI-generated movies have premiered. They were made for TCL, world's biggest manufacturer of TVs

TCL made them for their streaming channel TCL+, after studies showed their viewers don't like to change the channel once they have it on

The films were 5 AI-generated shorts:

One about a woman who turns into a slug (presumably one that doesn't like to change the channel)

Another put an actor into famous movie scenes via deepfake technology

Another was about a girl who wins a futuristic lottery where seeing the sun for the first time is the prize (probably another non-channel-changer)

Another was a superhero movie

And one was a documentary about a mountaineer who lost his leg in an avalanche (should've stayed home watching TV)

The films have been described as error ridden, ugly, and vacant-souled. TCL's chief content officer countered those accusations this way: "There are just as many continuity errors in major live-action film productions as there are in AI, and it's probably easier to fix in AI than live action"

Panic Room director David Fincher has used AI to remaster his film *Seven* for new home video release. He made shots of Kevin Spacey in the back of a cop car less blurry

ScreenRant writer Alexis Zaccaria reports it this way: "Fincher's efforts vitalize his commitment to preserving *Se7en*'s legacy as a cinematic classic. … By addressing past technical flaws, the remaster remains accessible to modern viewers who expect technical precision. … While the original film's imperfections may have gone unnoticed by many viewers, this remaster ensures the film's narrative is complimented by technical excellence"

Apple is discontinuing production of its VR Vision Pro headset rig—even though as we learned in the *Guardian* last week, VR has been perfected

Apple TV+ offered a free-streaming weekend for its catalog of original movies and TV shows

WBD, as a holiday surprise, put all of Stanley Kubrick's 1975 movie *Barry Lyndon* on YouTube for free, but neglected to include large parts of the film's score

The Sting, from 1973, is now the oldest movie on Netflix, one of only five on the platform made before 1980

Unfortunate Headlines of the Week:

"Linda Lavin Died with 3 Episodes Left to Shoot for New Hulu Comedy Series *Mid-Century Modern*"

"*Tango & Cash* Is Still Flawed yet Entertaining 35 Years Later"

"*A Complete Unknown* Is Knock-Knock-Knocking on the Door of an Elite Global Box Office List"

Note to headline writers: please stop with the "[Actor in some forthcoming movie] Is the Energy We Need in 2025" headlines

A writer for *Slate* worried that *A Complete Unknown* would ruin her love for actor Timothée Chalamet because Bob Dylan is gross

The donkey in *Shrek* was somehow based on a real donkey, and that donkey died this week at age 35

Justin Baldoni and his publicists and producers are now suing *The New York Times* for $250 million for "cherry-picking" and "stripping of necessary context" and "splicing to mislead" in the paper's coverage of actor Blake Lively's accusations against him for harassing her during the making of *It Ends with Us*

I am suing *The New York Times* for the cost of one copy of the paper for publishing an article with the headline "You Didn't Know Pam Anderson Is a Cinephile" and then only having one quote in it from her about movies she likes

It was revealed that Charli xcx has a Letterboxd account. It was immediately called "iconic" for reviews such as the singer's five-star review of Joel Coen's *The Tragedy of Macbeth*: "watched this whilst george built lego"

Elon Musk took to his X microblogging platform to praise inventor Nikola Tesla with a photo of *Juror #2* actor Nicholas Hoult as the inventor in the 2017 movie *The Current War*

Use of "murderous verbs" in films has surged over the last 50 years, a new study shows

In 2013, the (alleged) Las Vegas bomber Matthew Livelsberger was a contestant on a History Channel reality TV show called *Ultimate Soldier Challenge*

January 12, 2025

THE FIRES

In what is proving to be the largest and most devastating man-made "natural" disaster in US history, a series of catastrophic fires that began last Tuesday has engulfed Los Angeles and surrounding counties in flames. The deadliest of the fires, the Palisades and the Eaton fires, continue to burn, and are less than 30% contained as of this writing. Hundreds of thousands of people remain under evacuation orders

At least 16 people have lost their lives. Some of the dead are disabled people who were unable to evacuate. Upward of 15,000 homes and other structures have been destroyed, and the Westside neighborhood of Pacific Palisades has been razed, with 24,000 acres burned. The situation is the same in much of Malibu

Winds remain strong and are expected to continue through the middle of this week, potentially spreading fires or reigniting ones that have been put out

Damaged areas are larger than all of San Francisco or Manhattan

Dozens of architecturally significant houses and historical sites have been lost to the fires, including the Will Rogers ranch and museum and the Arnold Schoenberg archive

Rents and housing prices are expected to balloon in already unaffordable Los Angeles starting right away

Los Angeles and the fires are caught in the leadership vacuum that is American politics, with the sitting president doddering, useless, and quiescent, and the incoming one vituperative, scornful, and moronic. Local politicians have also come off unprepared and inadequate, despite the constant and heightened presence of wildfires in California last year

Republican Congressman Warren Davidson of Ohio has called for disaster relief to be withheld from California

As the fires worsened, social media became a site of absurd, privileged behavior. A multimillionaire real estate investor named Keith Wasserman, who is opposed to property taxes, asked for someone "with access to private firefighters" to protect his Pacific Palisades home. "Need to act fast here," he tweeted. "All neighbors houses burning. Will pay any amount"

Don't Look Up screenwriter and professional Democratic Party noodge David Sirota took to social media to blame film critics for the fires because they didn't like his and Adam McKay's Netflix movie. "The city of Los Angeles is a raging inferno less than three years after a bunch of elite pundits and film critics insisted *Don't Look Up* was too heavy handed and too unsubtle about the climate crisis," he wrote

Amazon Fresh food deliveries continued as the fires raged, as news photographs showed

Director Bryce Wagoner, who makes the film series *After Porn Ends*, refused to leave his home as the fires got nearer because he was waiting for a $300 Amazon Fresh delivery

NPR sponsorship ads asking listeners to consider Disney's *Inside Out 2* during awards season continued throughout radio coverage of the fires

Images of AI-generated white fireman with movie-star looks appeared on social media even though many of the firefighters are imprisoned convicts working for $26 a day. Up to 44% of CAL FIRE's force is made up of prisoners

International crews of firefighters from Canada and Mexico have arrived to help

Many celebrities, including some who own second homes in the area (and third and fourth homes elsewhere), have lost their houses in the fires, including in no particular order Candy Spelling, Paris Hilton, Heidi Montag and Spencer Pratt, Adam Brody and Leighton Meester, Anna Faris, Eugene Levy, Billy Crystal, Jeff Bridges, Rosie O'Donnell, Cary Elwes, Melissa Rivers, Ricki Lake, Milo Ventimiglia, Denise Crosby, Anthony Hopkins, John Goodman, Miles Teller, and Bozoma Saint John

The actor Henry G. Sanders, who starred in the 1978 Charles Burnett film *Killer of Sheep* and lives in the more affordable neighborhood of Altadena, is perhaps more representative of the people who have lost homes in the fires, despite intensive media coverage of Paris Hilton's loss, which has already been the subject of a story on *Architectural Digest*'s website

Earlier in the week basic news coverage included stories with headlines like "Ashton Kutcher Tries to Protect Friend's House from Wildfire with Garden Hose." Those have dissipated somewhat, but not entirely

Videodrome actor and MAGA shouter James Woods appeared on CNN weeping over the loss of his home, but later it turned out his property had been saved

Chet Hanks, the ne'er-do-well son of Tom Hanks and Rita Wilson, posted a moving message on Instagram, writing that "The neighborhood I grew up in is burning to the ground" and that he "Never thought the last time I drove thru my neighborhood would be the last time I ever laid eyes on it. Everything just memories now." "Pray for the Palisades," he added

Actor-director-madman Mel Gibson, who announced this week that he would make a sequel to *The Passion of the Christ* called *The Resurrection of the Christ* and that it would be "an acid trip," also lost his home

Gibson seems to have found out about the destruction of his home while he was in Austin, Tex., appearing on Joe Rogan's podcast. "I've been relieved of the burden of my stuff," said the *Apocalypto* director

Returning to Malibu, the *Road Warrior* star compared his property to Dresden after the bombings in World War II, saying "I have never seen a place so perfectly burned, you could put it in an urn"

Announcement of this year's Oscar nominations has been pushed back by two days

A screening of the 1980s music documentary *The Decline of Western Civilization* at LA film venue Now Instant Image Hall was canceled

EVERYTHING ELSE

The Penske-owned Golden Globes, held two days before the fires began, were heavily covered in the Penske-owned press

Golden Globes ratings were down, despite an inflated ratings comparison released by Penske

Former MoviePass Chairman Ted Farnsworth has pleaded guilty to defrauding investors in the company, and for conspiracy in claiming to have started a video-sharing platform that didn't exist

Eyebrowless OpenAI CEO Sam Altman is being sued by his sister, who claims he sexually abused her

A company in Dubai led by Hussain Sajwani has promised to invest $20 billion in US data centers, which of course lead to water depletion, electrical-grid failure, and more wildfires

Spanish *Emilia Pérez* star Karla Sofía Gascón, criticized for a myriad of reasons including her Mexican accent in the Netflix film, told a journalist that "Every Mexican I've met, except the one sitting in front of me, has said that my accent was impressive. If I were to speak in my typical accent to you, you'd die"

Playwright and actor in the Netflix TV series *Emily in Paris* Jeremy O. Harris has criticized members of the queer community who don't like *Emilia Pérez* and who have written against it, accusing them of "Pauline Kael cosplay," while stating that all queer movies should be supported because an unfriendly Trump administration is about to take power

Netflix has dumped *Asura*, a new TV series by Palme d'Or–winning Japanese auteur Hirokazu Kore-eda, onto their platform with no promotion or marketing

The British Labour Party's propolice TikTok ads feature large, AI-generated, reassuring, cute animals as cops who will make Britons "feel safer"

Due to complicated Academy of Motion Picture Arts and Sciences inclusivity rules, more than a third of Oscar-qualifying films this year are not eligible to be nominated for Best Picture

Amazon has paid $40 million for the Brett Ratner Melania Trump documentary, which will get a theatrical release. The soon-to-be-First-Lady-again is an executive producer on the film

Meta (Facebook) has deep-sixed its fact-checking program as a Trump ally, Dana White, a UFC executive accused of slapping his wife in public, has been appointed to Meta's board

Internal criticism of the move at Meta has been deleted from employee computers

Meta's Mark Zuckerberg announced this in a TikTok video while wearing a $900,000 wristwatch

Zuckerberg elaborated on his decision to Joe Rogan on Rogan's podcast, blaming the move on the Biden administration for censoring him, and ignoring Republican pressure on Facebook

Then Zuckerberg went to Mar-a-Lago to meet with Trump

Meta's Instagram announced it would begin showing users AI-generated versions of themselves. There was an immediate backlash against this from the public, and the company then announced it would throttle the program for now

Chen Pinlin, a Chinese documentary filmmaker who has been held awaiting trial for nearly a year, has been handed a three-year prison sentence for making a doc critical of the Chinese government's COVID lockdown. Chen is also known as Plato, and the film is called *Urumqi Road* in Chinese and *Not the Foreign Force* in English

An ex-Disney employee named Michael Scheuer, fired after he returned from paternity leave, has pleaded guilty to hacking into Disney menu-creation software to hide peanut-allergy information about menu items at theme park restaurants. Scheuer also changed wine-region designations to the locations of recent mass shootings, added swastikas to the menus, and locked his former coworkers out of their accounts

An actor named Keith Middlebrook, who appeared in *Iron Man 2* and claimed the TV series *Ballers* was based on his life, has been jailed for peddling a fake COVID cure he said was endorsed by basketball immortal Magic Johnson

After Earth actor Will Smith posted a message on Instagram implying he was to star in a new *Matrix* film, which is not the case

Peter Pan's Neverland Nightmare is the latest postcopyright horror movie based on a children's classic that became a Disney animated movie

The 2010s TV series *Grimm* will be rebooted as a feature film

Director Coralie Fargeat has promised not to make a sequel to *The Substance*

Disgraced *Call Me by Your Name* actor and accused cannibal Armie Hammer will star in prolific, disreputable director Uwe Boll's *The Dark Knight*, a "vigilante film"

Enter the Void director Gaspar Noé says he wants to direct a children's film

The Batman sequel *The Batman 2* has been pushed to 2027 because, according to producer James Gunn, "no one can accurately guess exactly how long a script will take to write"

Headline of the Week: "I Wanted an Old Republic *Star Wars* Series, but Now I'm Sure It Would Fail"

Social Network actor, playwright, feuilletonist, and film director Jesse Eisenberg has told *The Independent* that popularity in the film business is "transient," and that he is "in an unstable industry that doesn't care if you live or die." "I get my health insurance through my union," he added

January 19, 2025

My log does not judge

David Lynch has died at age 78

The great director of *Eraserhead*, *Blue Velvet*, *Twin Peaks*, *Lost Highway*, *Mulholland Drive*, *Inland Empire*, and others had been suffering from emphysema and related health problems and had to be evacuated from his home due to the catastrophic Los Angeles wildfires

Many of the 31 fires are still burning, including the massive Palisades and Eaton fires; the fires have claimed 28 lives; 205,000 people have been put under evacuation orders; air quality remains unhealthy; 65 square miles have now burned

This month's California wildfires are now the largest natural disaster / climate change event in US history

Bravo TV host Andy Cohen broke the news of Lynch's death on live TV to Patricia Arquette, the star of *Lost Highway*

Netflix co-CEO Ted Sarandos claimed immediately after Lynch's death that Lynch was working on a TV series for Netflix that "would have been his last project. It was a David Lynch production, so filled with mystery and risks but we wanted to go on this creative ride with this genius"

It was reported months ago that Netflix had passed on this and other Lynch projects

Nobody's Fool director Tyler Perry has criticized the "pure greed" of insurance companies who canceled homeowner policies in the Los Angeles area prior to the fires

In an Instagram post, the prolific producer-actor-writer-director asked, "Does anyone else find it appalling that insurance companies can take billions of dollars out of communities for years and then, all of a sudden, be allowed to cancel millions of policies for the very people they became rich on?"

Desperately Seeking Susan actor Rosanna Arquette has proposed that this year's Academy Awards ceremony be a 24-hour-telethon to raise money for the victims of the wildfires

She writes: "I woke up the other day thinking, 'What if we did a Jerry Lewis–style telethon but integrated it with the Oscars.' Imagine Billy Crystal opening the show. He lost his home, but he's the perfect person to unite the room"

Nickel Boys director RaMell Ross says he is open to talks with Marvel Studios to direct one of their superhero movies

Andy Muschietti, director of the 2023 superhero megaflop *The Flash*, says the would-be blockbuster failed because "it wasn't a movie that appealed to the four quadrants"

Muschietti added "I've found in private conversations that a lot of people just don't care about the Flash as a character"

Screenwriter Buck Woodall is suing Disney for $10 billion, claiming that *Moana* copied his 2003 screenplay for a movie called *Bucky the Wave Warrior* that was at one time to go into production at DreamWorks Animation

Bucky shares a number of elements with *Moana*: set in an ancient Polynesian village, teenage protagonist trying to save his land, ancient spirits in the form of animals, rooster and pig companions, a meeting with the Kakamora warrior tribe, and a whirlpool time portal

Barbie director Great Gerwig has somehow gotten Netflix to guarantee her forthcoming *Narnia* adaptation a full theatrical release with a long window before it goes to streaming

Don't Look Up director Adam McKay says that although "critics and cultural gatekeepers" hated his Netflix disaster movie, it was viewed by "400 million to half a billion" people on the streaming platform. Netflix has 283 million subscribers worldwide as of this writing. Probably 225 million of them invited friends over back in 2021 and 2022 to see the movie

Government Advisor Elon Musk tweeted an image of Will Ferrell in the Adam McKay movie *Step Brothers* to show that he and Amazon MGM Studios owner Jeff Bezos "just became best friends"

Mikey Shulman, CEO of AI company Suno, claimed in an interview that "It's not really enjoyable to make music now. It takes a lot of time, it takes a lot of practice, you have to get really good at an instrument or really good at a piece of production software"

He added that he thinks "the majority of people don't enjoy the majority of time they spend making music." Shulman says he wants to make making music accessible to "a billion people"

UK Prime Minister Keir Starmer says he wants to "mainline AI in the veins" of his nation, so that the UK becomes "the world leader" in artificial intelligence. I thought it already was

Social media enthusiast and screenwriter-director (*Oh, Canada*) Paul Schrader is claiming on Facebook that ChatGPT can come up with better movies in the style of himself, Quentin Tarantino, Harmony Korine, Ingmar Bergman, Roberto Rossellini, Fritz Lang, Martin Scorsese, F. W. Murnau, Frank Capra, John Ford, Steven Spielberg, and David Lynch than those directors can or could have come up with themselves. Schrader did not say what the ideas for these films that ChatGPT came up with were

I checked and this is not true, except in the case of Spielberg

TikTok briefly shut itself down, blaming the Biden administration for doing so, only to revive itself and thank incoming Trump administration for the save

President-elect Donald Trump has appointed Sylvester Stallone, Jon Voight, and Mel Gibson as "special ambassadors" to Hollywood. The former reality TV star says the three aging actors will "bring lost business back" to the film industry.

No word yet on what plans Trump has for the rest of the *Expendables* cast

Apocalypto director Mel Gibson claimed on Laura Ingraham's Fox News TV show that the LA wildfires are part of a plot to eliminate single-family homes in Los Angeles County and replace them with high-density housing. In a mélange of conspiracy theories, Gibson says that the drought and the Santa Ana winds "seemed a little convenient" and that perhaps arsonists were "commissioned" and not "acting on their own basis"

Stallone's new movie *Alarum* was released this week to bad reviews and a 0% Rotten Tomatoes score

New York employees of the Alamo Drafthouse chain are petitioning the company to not show the movie *September 5*, saying it is Zionist propaganda. The film covers TV coverage of the 1972 massacre of Israeli athletes at the Munich Olympics, and is expected to get Oscar nominations

Bollywood star Saif Ali Khan is recovering after having a knife removed from his back during surgery. The *Adipurush* actor was attacked in his Mumbai home on Thursday by an assailant who demanded 10 million rupees from Khan and has been detained

Director-actor-antimasculinist Justin Baldoni's lawsuit against Blake Lively is growing more ornate, as he is now asking that Disney preserve all material about the creation of the character Nicepool in *Deadpool & Wolverine*, saying it is a scurrilous portrayal of him

Baldoni's $400 million suit also claims that he and his family were held hostage in a movie theater basement during the New York premiere of his movie *It Ends with Us*, which stars Lively

Baldoni adds in the suit that *Cats* actor Taylor Swift pressured him to accept Lively's and husband Ryan Reynolds's rewrites of his *It Ends with Us* screenplay

In an even more sordid and depressing story that the Baldoni–Lively one, *Coraline* creator Neil Gaiman is newly alleged be a sexually abusive lunatic aided and abetted by his now ex-wife, singer and baby-doll-art enthusiast Amanda Palmer. Gaiman is also alleged to have not had a safe word

Disney recently stopped production on a Gaiman adaptation called *The Graveyard Book* because of previous allegations against the fantasy and comics writer

Robbie Williams's singing voice in *Better Man*, the biopic on the British singer in which he is depicted as a CGI monkey, was provided by singer Adam Tucker, and his speaking voice by actor Jonno Davies. The reason Williams didn't use his own voice is because he says he's too old to sound like himself anymore

The Hungarian accents of Adrien Brody and Felicity Jones in *The Brutalist* were partially created using AI tools. The reason this was necessary, according to those involved, is because Hungarian is a hard language to master. The film is in English

The New York Times twice published photographs of actor Glenn Strange as Frankenstein's monster, thinking they were photos of Boris Karloff

Shrek 5 has been delayed and will now swap release dates with *Minions 3*

Five Nights at Freddy's 2 is now shooting in Louisiana and *Five Nights at Freddy's 3* is already in the works and set for 2027 release

Napoleon director Ridley Scott will not be going ahead with his planned biopic of the Bee Gees

Sing Sing is the first movie released simultaneously in theaters and prisons

January 26, 2025

The Palisades Fire and the Eaton Fire continue to burn in Los Angeles, though they are now much smaller, and are joined by a new wildfire north of the city, the Hughes Fire

Donald Trump, the reality TV star and the actor who played "Waldo's Dad" in the 1994 movie reboot *The Little Rascals*, has been once again sworn in as president of the United States

The former and now present First Lady, Melania Trump, wore a hat to the inauguration apparently designed to make her look like Henry Fonda in *Once Upon a Time in the West*

Trump promises, among other things, to support the Stargate Project, a $500 billion initiative to build AI data centers across the country. The project is a joint venture of eyebrowless Napoleon-quoter Sam Altman's OpenAI, indoor golfer Masayoshi Son's investment company Softbank, future immortal Larry Ellison's Oracle, and an investment firm called MGX, which is the official AI investment company of the government of Abu Dhabi

The first of Stargate's data centers is slated to open in Abilene, Tex., by the end of the year. It will cost $1.1 billion to construct. The project is registered in Texas under the name "Project Ludicrous"

AI cloning was used in the Oscar-nominated movie *Emilia Pérez* to improve the singing voice of star Karla Sofía Gascón, because "it was necessary to increase the range of Gascón's vocal register"

With the announcement of this year's Oscar nominees this week, it is now officially "the Oscars have left the mainstream behind" think-piece season

Apocalypto director Mel Gibson says he was surprised to find out he had been named "special ambassador" to Hollywood by Donald Trump. "I got the tweet the same time as all of you," says Gibson, "and was just as surprised. Nevertheless, I heed the call"

Possibly the last Sundance Film Festival to be held in Utah has begun

Paramount has been served a legal letter forcing it to consider a last-minute, all-cash $13.5 billion offer from Project Rise Partners, in an attempt to stop Larry Ellison (not going to die) and Skydance Media from buying it

Project Rise Partners is headed by Daphna Edwards Ziman, president of lifestyle network Cinémoi, and Moses Gross, a real estate investor and venture capitalist, who are backed by a mysterious cabal said to include "at least one of the richest men in the world"

The Paramount Skydance acquisition had been a done deal for many weeks, after greedy National Amusements CEO and Paramount Chairwoman Shari Redstone accepted the Skydance offer

Government regulators may also block the Skydance merger anyway, because of an investment from a Chinese company called Tencent which is linked to the Chinese military

The New Yorker magazine is teaming with *Bubble* director Judd Apatow to make a documentary about itself for Netflix, which will be directed by a man who made a documentary about Cory Booker

Netflix claims to have added over 19 million new subscribers in the last quarter, and is now up to over 300 million, they say, claiming the big increase came from people signing up to watch the Logan Paul–Mike Tyson fight (I would like to meet one of those 19 million people)

To celebrate their big success, Netflix is raising their prices again, by $2 per plan, to $18 and $25 a month

Netflix also reiterates that starting soon they will decline to provide subscriber numbers

It now appears that higher prices, not greater attendance, are what's driving the Cineplex economic rebound (which I didn't even know about, as 2024 box office was reportedly down about 3.3% from 2023)

Sony is shutting down its recordable Blu-ray media production and will close its last factory in February

A TikToker on the street in Manhattan stopped and interviewed *Flight of the Intruder* actor Willem Dafoe without knowing who he was, asking him what he does for a living and where he sees himself in five years. The clip has garnered many views

American Gigolo actor Richard Gere has sold his Connecticut mansion and permanently relocated to Spain with his Spanish wife, Alejandra Silva, who is really Spanish. There the couple says they will work with the NGO Hogar Sí to end homelessness in Spain within five years

Some people going on YouTube are being subjected to ads that last from one hour to three hours before they can access the content they want to see. No one knows if this is a ploy to get people to subscribe to YouTube Premium or just a glitch with people who use ad blockers

Many people, not just intimacy coordinators and lawyers, have been analyzing the newly released outtakes from *It Ends with Us* of star Blake Lively and costar-director Justin Baldoni slow dancing and muttering to each other

Prolific voice actor Josh Gad says he was denied a role in *Avatar* because he's fat

It has crossed *Avatar* director James Cameron's mind, according to reports, "that we could be getting high on our own supply" in the making of *Avatar 3*

Headline of the Week: "Man in Spider-Man Costume Spills Milk on Self in Target Store in Social Media Stunt"

In other milk news this week, TruMoo has released a pink strawberry-banana *Moana* milk at supermarkets, in a "limited edition" that will be sure to appeal to milk collectors

The Luca Guadagnino *American Psycho* remake starring *Elvis* actor Austin Butler is not happening

A new CBS TV drama is called *FBI: CIA*

February 2, 2025

Eyebrowless OpenAI CEO Sam Altman began the week saying that his work selling AI to the world would require "changes to the social contract," and that "the entire structure of society will be up for debate and reconfiguration" because of what he and his company are doing

By midweek, Altman was whining that his multibillion-dollar plagiarism and misinformation AI software product was being plagiarized by the Chinese AI plagiarism and misinformation company DeepSeek, who released their own AI image generator, and made it open source, unlike that of OpenAI, a nonprofit organization with "open" in their name

He ended the week announcing that OpenAI has been "on the wrong side of history" because their AI model is not open source like the Chinese one

The DeepSeek AI product was developed for far less money than OpenAI's and uses much less energy than the climate-decimating OpenAI version

Because of DeepSeek's unexpected product release, chip maker Nvidia and other tech stocks, but mostly Nvidia, lost a trillion dollars in market value in one day. (Nvidia bounced back a bit the next day.) Valuation perceptions of OpenAI were needless to say also affected

DeepSeek was hit by outages after a major cyberattack in response to their announcement

New York Senator Chuck Schumer and others called this "a Sputnik moment." He says AI is a top priority in Congress, and that the US must not be beaten in the rush for better plagiarism- and misinformation-generating tools

Meta set up a "war room" of engineers to counter DeepSeek and figure out how they made their product so cheaply

Meta also this week settled a $25 million lawsuit with Trump over suspending his Facebook account

CBS is discussing settling its lawsuit with Trump, which asks for $10 billion over the editing of a *60 Minutes* segment Trump claims was misleading and pro–Kamala Harris

CBS is worried that if it doesn't settle there will be problems with parent company Paramount's merger with Skydance

President Donald Trump's embrace of AI has "exploded spectacularly in his face," writes website *Futurism*

Trump will meet with Nvidia CEO Jensen Huang to discuss things

AI researcher Steven Adler quit OpenAI, warning that the technology will quite possibly lead to the end of humanity, describing the pace of AI development as "terrifying"

The attorney general of the State of California has officially told AI companies that everything they are doing is probably illegal, not just because of the plagiarism but also because their practices are deceptive, their products are inaccurate and of low quality, and they have adverse effects on various protected classes of people

Chinese tech company Alibaba then released its own AI image generator that they claim is better than DeepSeek's

The tweet history of trans actor Karla Sofía Gascón—who has been nominated for an Academy Award for Best Actress for her work as the colead in the Netflix movie *Emilia Pérez*—has been revealed by Canadian journalist Sarah Hagi to include a large number of racist and other off-putting material going back years

The tweets, written in a sarcastic register, include bigoted comments on Muslims and anti-Islam slurs, anti-Black and anti-Asian comments mixed with attacks on an Academy Awards ceremony, a vicious insult to George Floyd, a dis to Gascón's *Emilia Pérez* costar Selena Gomez, who plays her wife-widow in the film, a weird homily about fat and skinny people and whales and dolphins and the nature of reality, an antilesbian remark that references the faith of Yatekomo, and last but not least, the sentiment that Hitler was right about the Jews

Gascón deleted the tweets and deactivated her X account

She then released a tepid apology referencing her Golden Globe Award acceptance speech, which involved light triumphing over darkness

Then had her lawyer send a cease-desist letter claiming that the anti-Gomez tweet was a fake

Then gave a rogue, tearful interview to CNN *en Español*, away from her Netflix handlers, in which she said, "I am not a racist," nor antisemitic, nor xenophobic

"What have I done in my life?" Gascón asked the interviewer. "I have not hurt a single fly. When I have a spider in my house I put a little glass on it so as not to kill it and take it out to the street"

Gascón added that this is a smear campaign, and that winning prizes is not a priority for her, and that what she really cares about is "the people that I represent"

Since *Emilia Pérez* premiered at Cannes last May, where it won the Jury Prize and Best Actress award from a jury headed by *Barbie* director Greta Gerwig, the film and Gascón have gone on to win 87 awards from various critical bodies and organizations

Gascón and the film garnered a near-record 13 Academy Award nominations, and have a number of awards nominations from other organizations pending

In other Selena Gomez news, the singer-actor posted an Instagram story of herself crying over ICE arrests in the US under Trump's new anti-immigrant orders. The *Emilia Pérez* costar then deleted it when right-wing trolls and politicians began to mock her by saying she should be deported herself

Gomez is a US citizen born in Grand Prairie, Tex.

"Apparently it's not OK to show empathy for people," Gomez posted in response, then deleted that, too, as the White House attacked her in a video posted on social media by White House Press Secretary Karoline Leavitt

Little Women actor Meryl Streep had to evacuate her Pasadena home during the Los Angeles wildfires by using wire cutters to make "a car-sized hole" in her garden fencing because a tree had fallen in her driveway

Rent gouging is now rampant in Los Angeles as the city recovers from the wildfires. Tenants are reportedly being overcharged a collective $93 million dollars a year. The rent increases cover units at all economic levels

The Prince Charles Cinema in London is facing closure because its landlord is insisting it has the right to alter the venue's lease

The film *Atropia*, directed by editor-writer-actor-model Hailey Benton Gates, has won the Grand Jury Prize in Drama at Sundance, despite taking a severe drubbing from the critics in attendance

Atropia takes place in a US Army training area set up to simulate an Iraqi village, and may be the final Iraq War movie

The Norwegian horror movie *Ugly Stepsister* reportedly caused at least one audience member to vomit into the aisle at its Sundance premiere

Nosferatu-remake director Robert Eggers will never make a contemporary-set film, he says, because "the idea of photographing a car makes me ill"

Captain America: Brave New World actor Anthony Mackie stated that "the term 'America'" should not be "one of the representations" associated with the Marvel superhero Captain America, whom he plays in the film

Mackie then apologized on Instagram stories, writing that he is a proud American, that playing Captain America is the honor of a lifetime, and that he supports the US armed forces

He went on to mention that he has given "at least four performances that should've been Oscar-nominated," one of which is apparently his lead role in 2004's *She Hate Me*

Adding that people "should chill the fuck out" over comparisons of the Red Hulk in the *Captain America* movie to Donald Trump

WBD DC honcho and *Suicide Squad 2* director James Gunn has defended a terrible-looking clip from his forthcoming *Superman* movie, saying that Superman's face does not look like an AI replacement at all, nor does it look goofy or cheap

The estate of one of Superman's creators, Joe Shuster, is suing WBD to stop the film from being released in British Commonwealth countries, citing a law that says the estate has copyright control in those parts of the world

The next James Bond, according to co-owners Amazon/MGM, will be campier so as to appeal to younger audiences

Lionsgate's Michael Jackson biopic is now in jeopardy well into shooting because producers forgot that certain aspects of Jacko's life were legally protected from on-screen depiction due to a settlement the singer reached with abuse accusers

British reality TV star Vicky Pattison is fighting deepfake pornography by making pornographic deepfakes of herself for a TV show called *My Deepfake Sex Tape* and releasing the X-rated material to the internet

Headlines of the Week:

"*Train Dreams* Review: Joel Edgerton's Western Drama Is Stunning to Behold & Yet I Just Couldn't Fall in Love with It"

"*Alien: Earth*'s Synopsis Already Has a Callback to James Cameron's *Aliens*"

Hans Zimmer, ubiquitous composer of Hollywood film scores and former Buggles keyboard player, has been hired by the Saudi Arabian government to punch up the country's national anthem

Nerve actor Dave Franco keeps telling entertainment news outlets that everybody tells him he looks just like Luigi Mangione

She-Devil actor Roseanne Barr released a pro-Trump rap video this week called "Daddy's Home"

Barr then announced she would star in a comeback TV show. She describes the possible four-to-six-episode series as "a cross between *The Roseanne Show* and *The Sopranos*" that centers on a family "saving the United States from drug gangs and China. They save America with guns, the Bible, petty crime, and alcoholism. It's kind of like the Coen brothers thing"

Death Proof director Quentin Tarantino says that "2019 was the last fucking year of movies," calling theatrical releases today "a show-pony exercise" designed to promote streaming platforms

When Harry Met Sally actors Meg Ryan and Billy Crystal appear in a TV commercial for Hellmann's mayonnaise in which they sit in Katz's Deli in Manhattan and reprise their roles from the 1989 romantic comedy as *Madame Web* actor Sydney Sweeney looks on

Hellmann's mayonnaise is certified kosher

Seville-based Spanish soccer team Real Betis Balompié released a video celebrating their acquisition of underperforming, single-named footballer Antony in a loan-out from Manchester United by releasing an AI-generated announcement video based on the work of David Lynch

The crap-looking video references *Twin Peaks* and *Blue Velvet*, among other works by the recently deceased master

For some reason, *Jojo Rabbit* actor Scarlett Johansson cohosted the *Today* show for four days last week on NBC TV

Ozempic left *Snatched* actor Amy Schumer bedridden, she reports

There is a great deal of Blake Lively–Justin Baldoni news this week, in their ongoing fight over their behavior while making *It Ends with Us*. A Baldoni voicemail has been released. *Cats* actor Taylor Swift is "stepping back" from her friendship with Lively. Baldoni has announced he is "a flawed man." He has also put up a website detailing his legal case. The trial is tentatively scheduled for March 2026

Sylvester actor Melissa Gilbert moved from Los Angeles to New York because, she says, "LA wasn't a safe place for me to age"

Behind Enemy Lines actor Gabriel Macht has moved out of the US with his wife and children but won't tell anyone where to

Starz, à la Netflix, now offers on their streaming platform three different things called *Snowflake*, *Snow Cake*, and *Cake*, all on the same content grid

The 2000 Takashi Miike film *Audition* is getting a US remake, to be helmed by Danish director Christian Tafdrup, whose 2022 film *Speak No Evil* was remade by Hollywood last year

King of New York actor Christopher Walken has never owned a cell phone or sent an email

Mel Gibson comeback directorial effort *Flight Risk*, starring *Boogie Nights* actor Mark Wahlberg as a hijacker-assassin with male-pattern baldness, has received miserable reviews and is the Number One film in the country

Yet another article, this time in *The Guardian*, has taken *The Brutalist* to task for not pleasing architects and architecture writers

Studio executives are anxious that Paul Thomas Anderson's forthcoming movie, *One Battle After Another*, will be too "eccentric and bizarre"

February 9, 2025

Moviegoers are upset that the Nicole Kidman "We come to this place for magic" promo spot / introduction to cinema clip is no longer playing before movies at AMC Theatres

Connecticut State Senator Martin Looney, calling the ads that play before movies "an abuse of people's time," has introduced a bill that would require movie theaters in his state to post actual start times of movies at movie theaters

Lucas Shaw, the person who writes *Bloomberg*'s film-industry newsletter, wrote these two paragraphs in his publication last week:

"Despite being the most powerful entertainment company in Hollywood, Netflix still feels misunderstood. Before introducing an impressive and never-ending slate of new programming at an event in Hollywood this week, Chief Content Officer Bela Bajaria told a room full of journalists what she thinks they get wrong about the company"

Second paragraph, *not* quoting Bajaria: "Netflix makes quality shows. It makes original shows. And it isn't operating out of fear. The room of reporters seemed more interested in whether Netflix would release more movies in theaters"

Nvidia CEO Jensen Huang says that everyone should get an AI tutor "right away"

Republican Senator Josh Hawley of Missouri is introducing legislation that will criminalize the use of DeepSeek's AI product in the US and impose a $100 million fine and a 20-year prison sentence on anyone who downloads it

Google will join OpenAI in using AI for weapons and surveillance technologies, despite having pledged never to do so

Marvel Studios has released a clip of a fight scene from *Captain America: Brave New World*, which fans have said "looks like a TV show" and "looks so bad" and "was just bad"

Marvel Studios has come under fire for using AI in the poster for the forthcoming "retro" *Fantastic Four* movie, after people noticed fingers and faces in the art that looked AI-generated. The studio denies using AI for the poster

Many, many Super Bowl TV commercials this year feature movie stars touting AI—similar to the crypto touting by celebrities in Super Bowl commercials in 2022, which led to lawsuits, arrests, trials, and prison time for some crypto fraudsters

Social Network actor/playwright Jesse Eisenberg says he does not want people to associate him with Meta CEO Mark Zuckerberg, whom he played in the 2010 film about the founding of Facebook

Over the last three months of 2024, Disney lost 700,000 subscribers to its streaming service, Disney+, and is predicted to lose more throughout 2025. Price hikes are to blame

Disney honcho Bob Iger says the losses don't matter, because theatrical revenue was so high thanks to *Moana 2*, which is currently part of a $10 billion plagiarism lawsuit

Disney has also mentioned that they are increasingly worried the cost of Disney theme park vacations is now out of reach for most Americans

The *Emilia Pérez* Affair continued unabated this week. First it was revealed that the Oscar-nominated colead in the movie, Karla Sofía Gascón, had excused herself from all awards-season events and functions, including ones at which she had been nominated for a prize

Next, Netflix, US distributor of the film, distanced themselves from Gascón, and is no longer footing the bill to bring her along to awards shows and other promotions

Gascón then announced she would also shut up about all this, saying she hopes her "silence will allow the film to be appreciated for what it is," adding that she continues to support her costars "200%"

A Spanish publisher that had planned to republish a 2008 "revised biographical novel" by Gascón canceled plans to do so

Emilia Pérez director Jacques Audiard called Gascón's racist tweets "hateful" and "inexcusable," saying reading them "was like falling into a hole." He has not discussed them with Gascón, he said, then responded to criticisms aimed at the film by announcing, "This is an opera, not a criticism of anything about Mexico"

The Alamo Drafthouse chain of quiet eat-in theaters has laid off much of the staff of its Denver-area locations

Unionized New York City Alamo Drafthouse workers are suing the chain for unfair labor practices in laying off NYC staff, saying the chain failed to bargain in good faith

Damien Leone, director of the *Terrifier* series of horror movies, has responded to backlash against actors David Howard Thornton, who plays Art the Clown in the films, and Lauren LaVera, who plays a cocreep in the movies, for their anti-Trump and pro-LGBTQ social media posts

Leone did not defend them, instead writing "*Terrifier* is not in any way shape or form a political franchise"

"I did not get into filmmaking," Leone continued, "to become a politician or promote any political agendas or ideologies, especially through a killer clown movie. I fell in love with horror movies as a form of pure entertainment"

Guess he hasn't seen the genre films of that other Leone who made *Once Upon a Time in the West*

Princess Bride actor/playwright Wallace Shawn says that Israeli treatment of Palestinians in Gaza is no different than what happened in Nazi Germany and is a genocide

Boycotts of the upcoming Berlinale continue, with Palestinian filmmaker Abdallah al-Khatib and Irish screenwriter Alan O'Gorman saying they will not attend despite invites. Both stand with Film Workers for Palestine and Strike Germany against German support of Israel and German censorship laws

Walmart has purchased the Monroeville Mall outside of Pittsburgh that was the filming location of George A.

Romero's 1978 film *Dawn of the Dead*, for $34 million. The mall is host to a Living Dead Museum and features a bust of Romero in the lobby

Coraline writer Neil Gaiman and his ex-wife, baby-doll-art enthusiast Amanda Palmer, are now being sued for the human trafficking of their babysitter

The Justin Baldoni–Blake Lively lawsuit situation continued apace last week. Now Lively is being sued by "crisis specialist" Jed Wallace of Street Relations, Inc., in a new *It Ends with Us* legal action. Wallace seeks $7 million for defamation, saying Lively falsely accused him of launching a "retaliatory campaign" against her

Headlines of the Week:

"*Jeanne Dielman, 23, Quai du Commerce, 1080 Bruxelles* Review—Sex, Secrets and the Unbearable Silence of Loneliness"

"All 7 Upcoming Barry Keoghan Movies Explained"

"How Would Bridget Jones Navigate Gen Z's New York City?"

The New York Times published a piece on the Frederick Wiseman retrospective at Lincoln Center this week under the headline "What an Instagram Reel Has in Common with a 4-Hour Documentary." The answer to the question is that "humans love to watch other humans"

At the same time as the *Times* published this example of goo talk, the paper noticed a trend of Gen Z audiences laughing and tittering during serious, sexy, and/or violent scenes in movies that are not comedies

Dune director Denis Villeneuve will make *Dune: Part Three* next, instead of the smaller feature he'd been planning. Reason? He "was really moved by the way *Part Two* was received by cinephiles around the world" and he "felt an appetite and a desire to see more and a responsibility to finish that story"

Actor Vin Diesel says he is eager to bring the *Fast & Furious* movies back to Los Angeles after the wildfires decimated parts of the county, so he has reunited with franchise costar Michelle Rodriguez to make a *Fast & Furious*–themed Häagen-Dazs ice cream TV commercial filmed on the Pacific Coast Highway

Back to the Future screenwriter Bob Gale says "Fuck you!" to anyone who thinks there should be a third sequel to the 1985 movie. Instead, Gale is concentrating on a Broadway-musical version of the film

Nomadland director Chloé Zhao will helm a *Buffy the Vampire Slayer*–reboot TV series for Hulu

The documentary *Last Time: Rust and the Story of Halyna* will premiere on Hulu in March. Halyna Hutchins's husband Matthew is an executive producer on this project about *Rust* star and producer Alec Baldwin fatally shooting his wife

Kash Patel, Trump's pick for FBI director, was paid $25,000 to appear in a documentary by Russian American documentary filmmaker Igor Lopatonok, who has ties with the Kremlin and has had films funded by Vladimir Putin. The doc series is called *All the President's Men: The Conspiracy Against Trump*

President Trump has called for the CBS TV news series *60 Minutes* to be "terminated"

Netflix has officially canceled release of its nine-hour Prince documentary, giving in to the wishes of the late Purple One's estate

Bones and All director Luca Guadagnino is now saying he will direct Stanley Kubrick's never-realized film *The Aryan Papers* for WBD

WBD, with no marketing, has just put over 30 movies on YouTube for free (with ads), including *Waiting for Guffman*, *Crossing Delancey*, *The Science of Sleep*, and *True Stories*. No one knows why, exactly, but it is presumably for the digital ad revenue from YouTube, technically a WBD competitor

Universal Studios has shelved the Pharrell Williams feature *Golden*, a collaboration with *Science of Sleep* director Michel Gondry, opting for a $20–$30 million loss. It was Williams and Gondry who pulled the plug, not Universal, despite the film being nearly complete in postproduction

The special popcorn bucket for the forthcoming horror movie *The Monkey* is said to be the "best design yet" for a novelty movie popcorn bucket

Multibillionaire Microsoft honcho Bill Gates says that although he has donated at least $100 billion to charitable causes over the years, he did it with no sacrifice to his way of life, adding "I didn't order less hamburgers or less movies"

Superman actor Henry Cavill's failed James Bond audition tape has leaked

Rupert Holmes's "Escape (The Piña Colada Song)" will be turned into a live-action movie by Alloy Entertainment

It is a testament to the negative relevance of the Sundance Film Festival that one of the biggest stories out of Utah last week was that a 17-year-old in Provo was arrested and faces charges for taping fish to ATM screens thirteen separate times, in the style—perhaps inadvertently—of Maurizio Cattelan's banana sculpture, *Comedian*

The teen committed these crimes last summer and fall, and his Instagram bio reads "Live, laugh, tape fish on ATMS"

The fish were trout, and he sometimes taped on three of them per ATM screen

Ex-president Joe Biden has resigned with talent agency CAA

February 16, 2025

Netflix has released a romantic comedy called *La Dolce Villa*

Bela Bajaria, chief content officer of Netflix, gave a long interview to *Puck* in which she called the revelation of *Emilia Pérez* star Karla Sofía Gascón's racist tweets "a bummer," said it was impossible to vet the social media of the tens of thousands of people who work on movies for Netflix, asked "What is prestige TV?," fudged the truth about the theatrical window of *Barbie* director Greta Gerwig's forthcoming Netflix *Narnia* movie several times, and repeated the infamous Netflix talking point that *Oppenheimer* would have done just as well had it been a Netflix release, citing Amazon's *Red One* as an example of theatrical and streaming success comparable to the success the Nolan movie would have had had it been made by Netflix

Titanic actor Kate Winslet will make her directorial debut with the Netflix movie *Goodbye June*, a family drama

Pearl Harbor director Michael Bay directed a TV commercial for the United States Secret Service that aired during last week's Super Bowl

Vice President JD Vance told world leaders that regulation could kill AI, and that it must be "free from ideological bias"

French President Emmanuel Macron then announced that France would pledge $112 billion in investments to bolster the French AI sector, matching what Trump is doing in the US

The first-ever AI image to be granted copyright protection depicts a woman's face made of stained glass, with a third eye and spaghetti for hair. It is called *A Single Piece of American Cheese* and was made by Kent Keirsey, founder of a generative-AI platform called Invoke

Guy Bar, the Israeli founder of an "AI tech hub" called Elevaitor [*sic*] cocreated a video filled with AI-generated Jewish actors and directors, used without their permission, to protest *Jesus Is King* actor-rapper Kanye West's recent anti-Semitic rants, social media posts, T-shirts, and TV commercials

The actors and directors, depicted wearing an anti-Kanye T-shirt, included David Schwimmer, Steven Spielberg, Jerry Seinfeld, Adam Sandler, Sacha Baron Cohen, and Scarlett Johansson

Black Widow actor Johansson responded by saying, "We must call out the misuse of AI, no matter what its messaging, or we risk losing a hold on reality"

Bar, creator of the video, defended it thusly: "It had to be [done] very, very fast. If you take time, it wouldn't be relevant. You must make very quick decisions. They are very famous. They are the most famous Jewish [people] in the world. They are very relevant to Kanye West's world. In a perfect world, the real [actors and directors would be] doing it with their voice. I wish they would share it and say, 'We definitely agree with this video, we want to spread it all over'"

A study commissioned by Microsoft found that using AI makes people stupider by eroding critical thinking skills

News agency Thomson Reuters has won the first major anti-AI copyright case. A US circuit court judge found that an AI start-up called ROSS Intelligence illegally reproduced material owned by Thomson Reuters's law-research division in creating its AI product. Said Judge Stephanos Bibas, "None of ROSS's possible defenses holds water"

Judge Bibas's decision is seen to reject as irrelevant all fair use arguments cited by AI companies

Problemista actor Tilda Swinton gave a speech at the Berlinale decrying "internationally enabled mass murder" and "greed-addicted governments who make nice with planet wreckers and war criminals." Swinton attended the festival to pick up her lifetime-achievement award and explain that she admires and respects BDS

Disney will change the content warnings they place before certain older films, in response to Trump's anti-DEI initiatives. The films include *Peter Pan* and *Dumbo*

The warnings had informed viewers that the films included "negative depictions and/or mistreatment of peoples and cultures."

They will now say the movies are "presented as originally created and may contain stereotypes or negative depictions"

Disney has created a variety of products for the 75th anniversary of the movie *Cinderella*, including a $7,000 diamond engagement ring, Starbucks tumblers, and white platform Crocs for tweens

The movie *The Monkey* was not allowed to depict the titular toy monkey crashing cymbals in its hands because the monkey-with-cymbals toy was copyrighted by Disney after it was used in 2010's *Toy Story 3*, despite having been introduced into the marketplace as Hoppo the Waltzing Monkey by toy maker Louis Marx & Co. in 1932 (see also James Bond story, below)

The Department of Justice shuttering its Kleptocracy Initiative unit evidently means that money seized from Riza Aziz, the financier of the 2013 Martin Scorsese movie *The Wolf of Wall Street*, will go to fund Trump's new immigrant internment camp on Guantánamo Bay

Bridget Jones: Mad About the Boy, the fourth Bridget Jones movie starring Renée Zellweger, opened to great reviews in theaters across the world this week, except in the US, where it debuted on the streaming service Peacock

Streaming service Hulu has let it be known that "certain titles and types of content" will now include ads, even in their "'no ads' or 'ad free' subscription tiers"

Unfortunate Headlines of the Week:

"Everyone Knew *Captain America: Brave New World* Was Not Going to Be a Good Film"

"*Captain America: Brave New World* in '5D' Is a Glorious Way to Celebrate a Mess of a Movie"

"It's Official: Doctor Doom Is Smarter Than the Avengers and the Fantastic Four Combined"

"*How to Train Your Dragon* Fans in Tears as Anticipated Remake Trailer Drops"

"10 Problematic *Harry Potter* Scenes That Don't Hold Up on Rewatch"

"The Green Gummy Bear from the Decades-Old Viral Internet Song 'Gummibär' Is Getting a Theatrical Feature"

The Washington Post went there, in their *Parthenope* review: "Say Nope to *Parthenope*"

James Bond is all of a sudden in a legal battle to keep use of that name. A Dubai-based property developer from Austria named Josef Kleindienst has filed a claim in the UK and in the EU saying that the owners of the trademark, the Broccoli family's companies Eon and Danjac and Amazon MGM Studios, are not using the name across a range of goods and services and therefore should not own it

Kleindienst seeks ownership of the name and "007," as well as the phrase "Bond, James Bond," and wants to use these on automobiles, computer programs, comic books, restaurants, cocktail lounges, and hotels

His claim is based on a European law that says if an owner does not commercially exploit a trademark for a period of five years, then a challenge to revoke ownership of a name can be made

Wildcat actor Maya Hawke, the daughter of actors Ethan Hawke and Uma Thurman, has expressed outrage that some movie producers now hire actors based on the number of social media followers they have

Goonies 2 (*Old Goonies*) is now officially in the works

There will be *Cape Fear* and *Boys from Brazil* miniseries

Fans are making their own special popcorn buckets to use during the release of Marvel's forthcoming *Fantastic Four* movie

Category fraud in Oscar nominations is high this year, with *A Real Pain*'s Kieran Culkin, *Emilia Pérez*'s Zoe Saldaña, and *Wicked*'s Ariana Grande all nominated for Best Supporting Actor Oscars when they are in fact coleads in their films

For Valentine's Day, music-industry person Benny Blanco presented his fiancée, *Emilia Pérez* actor Selena Gomez, with a trail of tortilla chips leading to a bathtub filled with melted cheese. The chips spelled out "I LOVE YOU"

This display was evidently not a tableau vivant illustrating the Emilia Pérez Oscar campaign

Gomez said of *Emilia Pérez* this week that "some of the magic has disappeared"

February 23, 2025

First Lady Melania Trump is selling $10 million dollar sponsorships for the documentary about her life that Amazon already bought for $40 million

$28 million of that $40 million was a fee Melania had already been paid

The sponsorships are being offered to CEOs, whose names will be included in the credits should they cough up

Vox Lux director Brady Corbet says he has made $0 on *The Brutalist*, and that other Oscar-nominated directors this year can't pay their rent

The other Best Director nominees are Sean Baker for *Anora*, James Mangold for *A Complete Unknown*, Coralie Fargeat for *The Substance*, and Jacques Audiard for *Emilia Pérez*

Corbet blames time-consuming press tours for his lack of earnings

Inherent Vice actors Martin Short and Maya Rudolph are among those who got COVID while appearing on *SNL50*, NBC's massive televised celebration of Lorne Michaels and *Saturday Night Live*

Logan Lucky actor Daniel Craig has quit *Bones and All* director Luca Guadagnino's *Sgt. Rock* movie for DC Studios. Reportedly Craig has soured on Guadagnino after Guadagnino's *Queer*, in which Craig starred, tanked at the box office and didn't make a showing during awards season

In other James Bond news, the Broccoli family has finally thrown in the towel and conceded full control of the Bond franchise to Amazon MGM

This has cost Amazon an additional $1 billion in payment to the Broccolis

Netflix is distancing itself from the origin story of their signature "tudum" sound, which is also the name of their promotional blog

The sound comes from Kevin Spacey knocking on the Oval Office desk in an episode of the Netflix TV series *House of Cards*

Netflix, backing away from Kevin Spacey, his legal problems, and his weird tweets about onetime *L.A. Confidential* costar Guy Pearce, says it doesn't come from that

Director Shiori Ito will recut her Oscar-nominated documentary *Black Box Diaries* to appease the petty legal concerns of various men so that the film can be shown in Japan, its country of origin

Unfortunate Headlines of the Week:

"7 Spider-Man Appearances You Completely Forgot About"

"All Hulk Colors in the MCU Explained"

Just Because You Write Headlines for Highbrow Movies Doesn't Mean You're Making Sense Either (Unfortunate Berlinale Headlines of the Week):

"*Kontinental '25* Shows Radu Jude Has Nothing Left to Prove"

"*Blue Moon*: Another Precious Pearl in Richard Linklater's Chronicles of the Human Condition"

In *It Ends with Us* controversy news, *Hotel Artemis* actor Jenny Slate filed an HR complaint while appearing in the Justin Baldoni–Blake Lively film because she found that the apartment she was renting while working on the movie was too small, and mentioned this to Jamey Heath, the president of the studio in charge of the troubled production

Heath told Slate he would reimburse her $15,000 security deposit so she could find a new place, but said so in a way Slate says made her uncomfortable

Welcome to the Dollhouse actor Eric Mabius has been arrested in a bar in Yulee, Fla., for spitting on people, pulling a woman's hair, and knocking two women to the ground. Mabius also stars in the *Signed, Sealed, Delivered* series of Hallmark movies

The *Rock 'Em Sock 'Em Robots* Mattel movie starring Vin Diesel is now in production

The Unbreakable Boy, released this week, was supposed to come out in 2022. It stars Zachary Levi, who is in the midst of a really remarkable three-year run of movies

Starship Troopers actor Denise Richards has an OnlyFans, and so does her daughter, Sami

The Alec and Hilaria Baldwin reality TV series *The Baldwins* has debuted. The show features Alec wringing his hands over his shooting of cinematographer Halyna Hutchins while making the movie *Rust*, Hilaria switching between her American and Spanish accents, antics from their seven children and two nannies

Defeated Democratic presidential candidate Kamala Harris has signed with CAA

Older AI models exhibit signs of cognitive decline, study shows

March 2, 2025

French Connection actor Gene Hackman, 95, and his wife Betsy Arakawa, 65, a classical pianist, have died at home in New Mexico, along with one of their three dogs, under mysterious circumstances

Authorities say foul play is not suspected but can't figure out what happened

Hackman and Arakawa were in separate rooms when they evidently collapsed

The deaths probably occurred on February 17, according to data from the *Royal Tenenbaums* star's pacemaker

Their bodies were found after a welfare check because friends, relatives, and neighbors had not seen or heard from them for some days

News media included details of the state of their corpses upon discovery

The Office of National Intelligence gifted its new director Tulsi Gabbard a Captain America shield to display in her new office as a member of Trump's cabinet

President Donald Trump posted a fake, AI-generated promotional video on his Truth Social platform for "Trump Gaza"—a post-war version of Gaza as a casino resort

The video's theme song includes the lyrics "Trump Gaza is finally here / Trump Gaza shining bright / Golden future / Brand new light"

Scenes in the video include Trump sunbathing with Netanyahu and partying with Elon Musk near a golden Trump statue

The pro-Israel company that made the video, run by Israelis in America Solo Avital and Ariel Vromen, claims the uniquely offensive and ugly video was satire

The big theater chains are threatening to withhold screening *Barbie* director Greta Gerwig's forthcoming *Narnia* movie because they dislike the deal IMAX struck with Netflix and Gerwig behind their backs

The Penske-owned Golden Globes has cut loose the do-nothing or do-very-little journalists of the Hollywood Foreign Press Association. These alleged writers will no longer collect their $75,000-a-year salaries from their Penske overlords. I fully expect great work to come from them now that they'll be hungry

The ceiling of a movie theater in Wenatchee, Wash., collapsed during a screening of *Captain America: Brave New World*. No one was hurt as there were only two people in the audience

Megalopolis director Francis Ford Coppola's defamation lawsuit against the Penske Media–owned publication *Variety* will be going to trial

The One from the Heart director also this week wrote an epic Instagram post after *Megalopolis* won Razzie awards, preempting that useless organization's announcement of the "winners" of their awards

Coppola's post is a tribute to filmmaking and a plea for art in a time of a beleaguered and hackneyed cinema and a wounded yet greedy film industry

The *Apocalypse Now* director wrote that he is "thrilled to accept the Razzie award in so many important categories," including Worst Director, Worst Screenplay, and Worst Picture

He concluded with the advice that we should "remind ourselves that box-office is only about money, and like war, stupidity and politics has no true place in our future"

Anora director Sean Baker called for higher upfront fees for directors, during his Spirit Award acceptance speech

Netflix founder Reed Hastings is opening a private ski resort at a public ski resort at Powder Mountain in Eden, Utah

Two thousand acres of previously public land will now only be available to residents of an area Hastings is calling Powder Haven, a members-only development

One hundred fifty plots have been sold there, for at least $2 million each, and fifty homes built

Five hundred more plots will be on sale by this summer, and the annual fee to own is $100,000 a year

What was left of Technicolor is shutting down because it can't find new investors

The company now just owns a bunch of VFX studios

Avatar director James Cameron is moving to New Zealand and becoming a citizen there. He says that the US under Trump is "horrifying"

Sony has taken out a patent for a process that will allow TV viewers to skip commercials if they yell the name of the product being advertised

Microsoft is canceling leases for AI data centers as Wall Street cites exaggerated demand

Alibaba is making its Wan2.1 text-to-video AI model free to use

Paper Moon actor Tatum O'Neal was left out of her father's will, she learned when Ryan O'Neal, her dad and *Paper Moon* costar, died in December 2023. Her response? "Keep it, motherfucker"

The *Bad News Bears* actor also says she "never really fully recovered from" her father not allowing her to audition for the Jodie Foster part in *Taxi Driver*

It appears that Film at Lincoln Center is settling a class-action lawsuit against them for $400,000. The suit charges the august institution with hiding fees on e-ticket sales

Nostalgic Headline of the Week: "Andrew Scott Passed a Kidney Stone at the 2020 SAG Awards"

History Buff Headline of the Week: "Researchers Puzzled by AI That Praises Hitler After Training on Insecure Code"

The Fox-owned streaming service Tubi, which is free and ad supported, had more streaming hours in 2024 than any other streamers besides YouTube and Netflix. It has the biggest content library of any streamer and its viewership grew by 50% last year

Nonetheless, Fox is creating a new streaming platform to compete with Tubi, unnamed at this time

Fox also turned down a $2 billion offer to sell Tubi

Blonde director Andrew Dominik's new film, this one for Apple, not Netflix, is *Bono: Stories of Surrender*, a documentary about the U2 singer the Mekons once described as "the Dublin messiah scattering crumbs"

The film will premiere in May with an "immersive version" available on Apple Vision Pro, the first film to be made available in this 8K format, which places viewers in a 180-degree environment on stage with the singer

This is, according to Apple, "in keeping with Bono's enduring commitment to innovation"

The film is based on Bono's memoir and one-man stage show

State Property 2 actor Kanye West debuted a $25 million Vanessa Beecroft nude film starring his wife Bianca Censori, who attended the premiere in a chador

The film focuses on how "shame over being naked is not natural to humans"

News reports I read did not include the title of this film, and I didn't look that hard to find it

Well-known and high-profile British musicians, including Annie Lennox and Kate Bush, released a silent album to protest AI use of their works

The album is called *Is This What We Want?*

It is part of the Make It F*AI*R campaign in the British press against UK-government proposals to allow AI companies to train their models on copyright-protected works

People got upset that *White Lotus* TV series actor Patrick Schwarzenegger got upset that he was called a nepo baby

It Ends with Us actor Blake Lively is upset with a *Hollywood Reporter* cover that depicts her and director-manchild Justin Baldoni dressed in biblical outfits fighting in a desert, where Lively is slingshotting an iPhone at the screenwriter-actor-author

Release of *The Lord of the Rings: The Hunt for Gollum* has been pushed back a full year by WBD, to December 2027

A Harry Potter store is opening in Chicago in April

Fans say Shrek looks old in the new *Shrek 5* trailer

March 9, 2025

A 3.9-magnitude earthquake struck Los Angeles as the Oscar ceremony was ending last Sunday night

After she won the Best Supporting Actress Oscar for *Emilia Pérez*, Zoe Saldaña made an attempt to apologize to Mexico for the film's racist approach to its setting. Instead, she ended up saying that the film was made "from a place of love" (France?) and that she didn't share the opinion of Mexicans offended by the film

Saldaña continued by explaining, "We were making a film about four women. These women could have been Russian, could have been Dominican, could have been Black from Detroit, could have been from Israel, could have been from Gaza. And these women are still very universal women that are struggling every day, but trying to survive systemic oppression and trying to find authentic voices" (using Respeecher?)

She concluded by saying she is "always open to sit down with all of my Mexican brothers and sisters, with love and respect, [to have] a great conversation on how *Emilia Pérez* could have been done better. I welcome it"

¡Esperando sentado, México!

Emilia Pérez director Jacques Audiard declined to make a trans-rights statement at the Oscars because, he said, "I didn't win"

After it was announced that Adrien Brody had won the Best Actor Oscar for *The Brutalist*, he took the stage to accept his award by throwing his chewing gum at his wife, Georgina Chapman, former wife of Harvey Weinstein, who has suffered enough, and then made a lengthy acceptance speech that should have had an intermission, like *The Brutalist* has (am I late to that joke?)

People on social media made a point of saying that they noticed who did not stand and applaud when *No Other Land* won the Oscar for Best Documentary Feature, but didn't bother to say who it was not standing or applauding

Israeli Culture Minister Miki Zohar called *No Other Land*'s Oscar win "a sad moment for the world of cinema" and said the film "is sabotage against the State of Israel," adding that this is why Israel does not support cinema

Rapper-singer Doja Cat says it was "brave and scary" to go out on stage at the Oscars to sing "Diamonds Are Forever" and not be able to carry a tune. "A bitch hit some flats," the "You Right" singer posted on social media, continuing "I can't wait to do something like that again"

Some fashion commentators claimed the naked-dress trend had peaked at the Oscar after-parties, citing *Booksmart* director Olivia Wilde's nightgown dress and *Uncut Gems* actor Julia Fox's hair-extensions-under-dress look

Former presidential candidate Kamala Harris was scheduled to attend the Oscars but pulled out at the last minute. The "new evolving security environment" in which we live was cited as the reason

Glitches on Hulu were blamed for driving Oscar telecast ratings down 7% from last year

No, they were up 1%

Neon spent $18 million marketing the $6 million film *Anora*

A court in Bangalore, India, has ordered a PVR movie theater to pay for the mental agony of showing too many ads before films start

The judge said that forcing paying customers to sit through half an hour of ads that begin at the scheduled showtime is "unjust and unfair"

The plaintiff sued because in December 2023 he rushed to the theater to be on time to see *Sam Bahadur*, then had to sit, breathless but fuming, through the ads

WBD CEO David Zaslav is upset about the money-losing movies his company has been releasing, implying they are too auteur driven; he doesn't want critical darlings making original projects with tentpole budgets

The former cable exec is said to be "losing patience" with the high art of movies like *Mickey 17* and *Joker: Folie à Deux*, a film he lavishly praised before release, and now thunders that Warners "must deliver consistency"

Village Roadshow, prestige production company that partners with Warners, is in a legal fight with WBD; the Writers Guild has issued a "do not work" order against Village Roadshow; the company is looking to sell its catalog of more than 100 films, including the *Matrix* movies, the *Ocean*'s movies, the *Lego* movies, and *Joker*

Warner Bros. DVDs made between 2006 and 2009 are rotting in their cases. Many are of classic films no longer available on home video. WBD has not explained the manufacturing glitch from those production years, though they have said they are aware of the problem

New Netflix mockbuster *The Electric State*, from the Russo brothers, starring Chris Pratt, Millie Bobby Brown, and Woody Harrelson as the voice of Planters brand icon Mr. Peanut, somehow cost $320 million to make and has debuted to a 10% rating on Rotten Tomatoes; viewers call it "a reductive amalgam"

The causes of death of *French Connection* actor Gene Hackman and his wife have been discovered. Hackman was suffering from Alzheimer's disease and a serious heart condition, and died a week after his wife Betsy Arakawa died of hantavirus while in the act of taking medications to treat her thyroid condition and high blood pressure

It is not known how Arakawa contracted hantavirus

Their dog, Zinfandel, a 12-year-old Australian kelpie that was also found dead at the scene in their New Mexico home, locked in a cage where it was recovering from surgery, may have died of starvation

Hackman's Alzheimer's evidently prevented him from grasping the situation, and from making any calls or otherwise seeking help in the week after Arakawa's death, before he collapsed and died himself

Amazon Studios is forcing Phoebe Waller-Bridge to do something in order to justify the multimillion-dollar deal she signed with them in 2019. The *Fleabag* creator and star will narrate a new documentary about an octopus

Monkey director Osgood Perkins says he would not direct a James Bond movie "because fuck Jeff Bezos"

Amazon MGM Studios head Bezos is reported to have become so angry after the Broccolis laughed off his idea for a Miss Moneypenny spin-off from the James Bond movies that he spent that extra billion to cut them loose

James Bond becomes public domain in 2035

Bambi: The Reckoning is the latest public domain horror movie based on a former Disney property

Even Dwarfs Started Small director Werner Herzog will make an animated movie called *The Twilight World* based on his novel about a Japanese soldier in the Philippine jungle who refused to surrender for 30 years after World War II ended

The animated film will tackle these themes: the nature of reality, the illusion of time, and the conflict between the external world and inner life

Disney has laid off 200 more employees, many of them from their ABC News division

Nate Silvers's 538 will be deep-sixed

As the result of a lawsuit Disney settled, *Good Morning America* coanchor George Stephanopoulos was forced to publicly apologize to Donald Trump for calling him a rapist when technically he is merely a "sexual abuser"

Pathetic Headline of the Week: "I Wore a One-Horsepower Exoskeleton to the World's Biggest Tech Show"

Ezra Edelman, director of the canceled Netflix Prince documentary, is calling out the trend of celebrity-documentary "slop"

Shark Tank actor Kevin O'Leary, a Canadian businessman and multimillionaire, plans to open Canada's biggest data center, in Alberta

Tron: Legacy actor Michael Sheen has bought off £1 million in personal debt for 900 people in South Wales

There will be a TV doc about it called *Michael Sheen's Secret Million Pound Giveaway*

Don't Worry Darling actor Florence Pugh says *Thunderbolts* is an A24 movie with MCU superheroes

An official town statue of Paddington Bear was stolen in Newbury, England. It was discovered sawed in half. Two 22-year-old men were arrested

The Batman actor Robert Pattinson says he can't watch horror movies anymore

March 16, 2025

This weekend continued the box office slide to Clinton-era numbers in attendance and revenue. At the same time, news outlets are declaring Netflix's $320 million boondoggle *The Electric State* a huge hit, despite its critical drubbing, simply because Netflix says it is the No. 1 film on their streaming platform, a meaningless statistic checked by no one and swallowed whole by the entertainment-news media

For instance, Ian Youngs of *BBC News* writes that "Critics' opinions have become irrelevant in the streaming age. The bad reviews didn't stop *The Electric State* from going straight to number one on Netflix's chart after its release on Friday. It fits into Netflix making star-packed, entertaining and escapist movies that often get panned by reviewers—but are watched by hundreds of millions of subscribers"

There is no actual evidence that "hundreds of millions of subscribers" watched *The Electric State*, a film this *BBC News* report calls "star-packed, entertaining and escapist" with no evidence the writer has actually seen it. Youngs also writes that these movies are "often panned" by reviewers. In fact, they are "always panned" by reviewers

Why is the BBC simply rewriting Netflix press releases? Surely Youngs at the very least knows Netflix counts a viewer playing a movie for even a few seconds in their tally of how many people have watched something?

Two groups in Sweden, Boykot varer fra USA and Bojkotta varor från USA, are asking their fellow countrymen to cancel their Netflix accounts because of Trump's tariffs on European goods and lack of support for Ukraine

Netflix has announced a remake of the 1983 Stephen King adaptation *Cujo*

Meanwhile, the floundering Marvel Studios is sending *Midsommar* actor Florence Pugh out to declare to the press that their new movie *Thunderbolts* has "badass indie" credibility, an approach reflected in the film's trailer, which references on-screen various indie films the actors and other craftspeople involved in making *Thunderbolts* have worked on

The ICE agent who arrested Palestinian graduate student Mahmoud Khalil in his Columbia University apartment for protesting against Israel was wearing a Marvel T-shirt

When reality TV actor Kim Kardashian traveled to India last year for the megawedding of billionaire scion Anant Ambani, she thought the country would remind her of the animated 1992 Disney movie *Aladdin*, which takes place in a fictional Middle Eastern city in the 14th century and is a cartoon

The cost of making the next two *Avengers* movies is expected to be over $1.3 billion. The films will shoot in the UK to get that 25.5% tax reimbursement

Disney held a low-key premiere for *Snow White* at a castle in Europe and then a small-scale premiere for the film in Hollywood, keeping stars Rachel Zegler and Gal Gadot away from the press, lest they say anything about their positions on the war in Gaza, or about how there are no dwarfs in the film, or about how huge the budget was, or about how it is a bad, unnecessary movie made for cynical IP purposes

Jumba and Pleakley will not disguise as a married couple in the *Lilo & Stitch* live-action remake, but will instead be played by *Hangover* actor Zach Galifianakis and some other guy in regular clothes

Miami Beach Mayor Steven Miner plans to end a movie theater's lease for showing *No Other Land*. The tiny movie theater, O Cinema, rents from the city and initially said they would not show the documentary on the forced Israeli evacuation of a Palestinian village. Then the movie won an Oscar

In a letter to O Cinema published in the *Miami Herald*, Miner calls the film "a one-sided propaganda attack on the Jewish people." He also branded it "inaccurate." There is no evidence he has seen the film

I Never Sang for My Father actor Gene Hackman's will left his entire estate to his wife, Betsy Arakawa, who died a week before he did. In turn, Arakawa left everything to Hackman in her will. Neither left anything to Hackman's three children

Delusional Headlines of the Week:

"*Power Rangers* Reboot Movie Is a Reminder of the Cinematic Universe We Lost Too Soon"

"Daisy Ridley Is Reinventing the Zombie Movie"

"*Star Wars* Tricked Us All with One of Darth Vader's Recent Iconic Kills"

Delusional Social Media Caption / Ad Copy of the Week:

"Experience the magic of AirPods 4 with Active Noise Cancellation in a film directed by Spike Jonze, starring Pedro Pascal"

Paramount, at some conference, revealed how they plan to use AI for content production, scripting, and other production tasks, saying that their business model has always been "text to video"

Jobs AI will perform for Paramount will include: script analysis for budgeting, finding B-roll in archives, assembling clips, editing in general, and generating actors' faces

Paramount has canceled the MTV Movie & TV Awards again this year

Eyebrowless OpenAI CEO Sam Altman has once again declared that the AI race is over if training on copyrighted material is not declared fair use in court and made into law

The billionaire visionary who runs a nonprofit corporation also, once again, called for a ban on "state-controlled," "PRC-produced" AI models

Altman is using AI to re-create an older technology: the broken record

Harry Potter actor Jessie Cave, who plays Lavender Brown in the film series, has started an OnlyFans account "to get out of debt" and "empower" herself

Her OnlyFans will feature ASMR hair sounds, which the *Great Expectations* actor says are not sexual in nature. "It's a fetish," she explains. "Fetish doesn't necessarily mean sexual"

There will be a *Quiet Place III* with auteur John Krasinski as soon as his schedule frees up from narrating and appearing in TV commercials

Yahoo Entertainment writes that the *Quiet Place* series is "now arguably considered one of the best horror franchises in modern cinema"

There is a *Starship Troopers* remake in the works from *Chappie* director Neill Blomkamp

New company headed by *Hostel* director Eli Roth called the Horror Section will allow fans (fans of what?) to invest in movies before they're made, share in the profits if Hollywood accounting practices determine there are any

Hereafter actor Bryce Dallas Howard, daughter of *Hillbilly Elegy* director Ron Howard, has made a documentary about pets for Disney+

Pets will feature "inspirational stories, archival footage, viral videos, and engaging interviews with children"

Says Howard *fille*, "Directing a documentary about the relationship between pets and people has been a dream for years"

Animated movie *Sneaks* will feature talking footwear

This is the final issue of Last Week in End Times Cinema

Afterword

Last Week in End Times Cinema began on March 17, 2024, a Sunday that also happened to be Saint Patrick's Day. I have the bad habit of reading entertainment news online every morning, which I picked up on an old job, and that day I'd noticed a number of stories from the world of movies that struck me as pathetic and ridiculous. Not just absurd, but also indicative of the postpandemic world of slop into which the film industry was descending, even as the CEOs running it were getting richer. I decided to list these items in an Instagram Stories post with a background of pink and green squares copped from Wikipedia filmographies, and I put it under the header *Last Week in End Times Cinema*.

The next week I noticed more film news that elicited the same kind of queasy rejection in me—the big No. Of course there was more. We are living through a time of great technological ruin and corporate destruction in the film industry, at all levels, from script development to theatrical exhibition to film journalism. So I posted those stories, too. I decided I would only post bad news in this now-weekly feature, only the very stupid and obviously wrong, things that were redolent of end times in a once-great industry and art form.

Stringing these stories together, I decided nothing would dilute my ire. I wasn't going to include things like Happy

Birthdays to directors or actors or anything like that. (Though on October 13, 2024, I did make a nod to the one hundredth anniversary of the birth of Edward D. Wood Jr.) I had to present everything naked, stripped of any ameliorating showbiz happy talk.

People seemed to like seeing this digest of tragic or trivial fatuity every Sunday in their Instagram feed. Meanwhile, I began noticing more and more stories I could include. After the fifth issue, I decided to email *Last Week in End Times Cinema* to people I would ask to subscribe in that week's post. It became a newsletter I emailed to whoever asked me to sign them up for it.

Soon I had hundreds of subscribers, because readers told their friends about it and gave them my email address, and later it was mentioned in *Puck*, which led to a few dozen new people emailing me asking to get it. The number of subscribers topped out at 996, I believe. It was hard to keep track and I had to send out each newsletter in several batches or it would crash my email client. I don't know how many people shared it with others once it landed in their inbox on Sundays.

I decided I would do *Last Week in End Times Cinema* for one full year. It would become an almanac of every bad thing that happened in the film industry from mid-March 2024 to mid-March 2025, an archive of unfortunate movie bulletins, an annual, presented in digest form and now collected in this book. A film-magazine editor I know told me it was a work of "hybrid criticism," a description I have come to embrace.

The customized batches of misfortune and upheaval in each newsletter recorded a full year of wrong thinking, bad decisions, and man-made disasters in the interlinked worlds of film production, film festivals, movie theater exhibition, streaming, and awards shows. And in the way they were reported in print and digital news media. Events unfolded in just this one year in ways I could not have foreseen but that now seem entirely inevitable in their mixture of crumminess and horror. Against the backdrop of the crazed push for AI, the wildfires in Los Angeles, the reelection of Donald Trump, the death of David Lynch, and the film industry's response or nonresponse to the war in Gaza, a picture of general disaster emerged, in a business defined by overpriced streaming platforms, sudden theater closures, and a dead-end reliance on intellectual-property franchises, most of them as tired as they were infantile. As Hollywood plunged into near irrelevance as a cultural force, these weekly roundups tracked every piece of bad movie news I could find, every easily avoided blunder, every up-to-the-minute example of unnecessary garbage as it emerged from the content mills of the newly tech-based film biz.

I presented it all without commentary—the selection was the commentary. Nor did I include footnotes or links. Félix Fénéon's *Novels in Three Lines* inspired me, in which the French fin de siècle anarchist and art critic who "only aspired to silence" wrote up violent news stories as tersely as he could. I wanted to combine his approach with the *Coffee News*, the free place mat–newsletter that is still found in some diners. Later I realized I was also inspired by the chalkboard of news items a liquor store in Brooklyn called Vine Wine places in front of their shop, then photographs and puts on their Instagram. The way I ordered the items came from the late novels of David

Markson. I wanted a definite narrative flow in their arrangement, the same way I order the short pieces on movies in my film-review columns for *n+1*.

I really didn't know what I was getting into when I decided to make a deep dive into entertainment news every morning. Before when I read it, I glossed over things of no interest to me. Now I stopped and looked. The fact is that the real movie news is not in the Entertainment or Arts sections anymore, but in the Business and Tech pages. The Entertainment section is now fully dominated by low-grade gossip, pseudoevents like trailer releases, idle speculation about people in talks with other people, and random nonreviews from nerdy websites that favor superhero movies above all else.

Anything interesting is found between romantic-relationship news about celebrities and semicelebrities and semifictional people. A certain singer-songwriter and her pro athlete boyfriend dominate this area (from today: "Taylor Swift and Travis Kelce 'Very Aligned' on 'Future' of Their Relationship: 'They're Really Happy'"). Stories about the British royals, appalling in American news in my opinion, take second place, followed by updates on reality TV series contestants ("'Beyond the Villa' Signs That *Love Island USA*'s JaNa Craig, Kenny Rodriguez Were Headed for a Split") and random items about obscure-to-me rich people getting engaged or married ("Why Eve Jobs' Wedding Dress Caused a Backlash from Locals").

Movie news isn't really reported news in the Entertainment section. Like so much in media, it now favors people's responses to things they've seen on TV ("I Expected *Happy Gilmore 2* Would Be a Fun Sequel, but Was Surprised by Who My Favorite Character Turned Out to Be"). Trailer-release reactions are now a subgenre all their own. It's often unclear whose reactions they are supposed to represent. A headline like "*Avatar: Fire & Ash* Trailer Officially Released Online: James Cameron Returns with Fiery Stunner" mixes the official status of an announcement from a studio's publicity department with a review: this film that doesn't exist yet is a fiery stunner.

I put together the *Last Week in End Times Cinema* newsletter with a certain kind of joy, but at a certain point the sheer cumulative repetition of this kind of nonnews, coupled sometimes with genuine tragedy (movie theater closures, the wildfires in Los Angeles, the deaths of Gene Hackman and his wife), began to get to me. Readers sometimes wrote me that the newsletter was depressing but also addictive. It was a doomscroll, one said, of a very specific kind, in a concentrated form, about one thing only.

A prominent figure, whose name came up week after week, was a particular source of depression. That was David Zaslav, the head of Warner Bros. Discovery, a lawyer from cable TV who somehow wormed his way into running a studio whose operations dated to 1903, when the actual Warner brothers started showing Edwin S. Porter's *Life of an American Fireman* and *The Great Train Robbery* at their movie theater in Pennsylvania. Zaslav has been deemed the most overpaid CEO in America. He called *The Flash*, a huge bomb for his company in 2023, "the best superhero [movie] he has ever seen." "I've seen it three times," he said. "It's a very emotional movie. You're going to go through all the emotions. … I think it's broken new ground. … It's very personal. It's very inspiring." Contrast that with a quote from Walt Disney I came across in the news the week of August 8, 2024. "I'm a born experimenter," Disney said in 1966. "To this day, I don't believe in sequels. I can't follow popular cycles; I have to move on to new things. There are many new worlds to conquer."

WBD paid David Zaslav $51.9 million in 2024, while the company is said to have lost $11.3 billion. Doing the opposite of ol' Walt is not good for a studio but it is good for its CEO. As I write this, WBD has announced it is splitting into two companies, Warner Bros. and Discovery, and that Zaslav is getting a pay cut. Zaslav will still head Warners, which this year has had a number of hits: the *Minecraft* movie, *Superman*, *Sinners*, *F1*, and a new *Final Destination* movie. With the exception of Ryan Coogler's *Sinners*, these are formula movies based on preexisting intellectual property.

According to *Variety*, a publication of Penske Media, which now owns all the major film-industry trade magazines and is heading toward monopoly status, "Zaslav has decided that WBD's future lies in streaming and HBO, along with the production studios that pump TV shows and movies into the streaming ecosystem." When a studio like Warners has hits, they still see them merely as ads for their afterlife in streaming. You can take the CEO out of cable television, but you can't take the cable TV content out of the CEO.

When executives like Zaslav talk about the future, they are speaking from a place of greed, but also cowardice. Their release slates of sequels, prequels, interquels, lega-sequels, reboots, and remakes show they are not risk-takers. Their goals are to offshore and eventually eliminate labor in domestic film production and to get rid of theatrical exhibition in favor of an all-streaming industry that replicates cable television at a higher price. Making TV shows is just easier, and cheaper. And getting rid of theatrical exhibition cuts out the middleman.

When I worked in television branding, there were two phrases I heard from studio executives every time I had to interact with them. One was that, first, before they did anything else, they had to go after "the low-hanging fruit." They never really defined what this low-hanging fruit was. They meant they had to keep making low-quality products for undemanding audiences because that was the easiest and least risky thing to do; it was guaranteed money in the bank. The other phrase was that making any kind of change at their company, even the smallest, was like "turning around a battleship."

Running, say, TBS required the skill and the patience of an admiral patrolling the seas in defense of our country, commanding a crew of thousands in a vessel that weighed seventy thousand tons. It was *military* in its logistics, and it was *heavy* and *big*. It wasn't just deciding when to schedule reruns of *New Girl* and figuring out where to put the ad breaks in a two-and-a-half-hour movie you were showing in a four-hour time slot. Because it was so complicated, change was impossible. Whereas picking the low-hanging fruit was easy, a simple matter of reaching up and plucking something that was about to fall into your basket on its own.

This mentality sums up the core business of the Hollywood studios today, which is making repetitive products aimed at lowest-common-denominator audiences in an atmosphere where no one is allowed to do anything else. If the year this book envelops proves anything, it is that now is the time to turn the battleship around. We are not in an orchard blossoming with ripe fruit. We're swirling in the Pacific Trash Vortex and the ocean is on fire.

Acknowledgments

Special thanks to Miriam Bale, Wick Hallos, Mark Krotov, Trish Lavoie, Funa Maduka, D. W. Mault, Hind Mezaina, Sarah Miller, Kate Perkins, Jenny Perlin, Suzanne Smith & Geoffrey Clark, Will Tavlin, and Anthony Volpe

A great thanks to the readers who donated money to *Last Week in End Times Cinema* while it was a weekly newsletter: Brad Abel, Stuart Adriance, Seth Allen, Michele Alpern, Brett Anders, Bill Arceneaux, Tom Augustine, Jon Auman, Brad Babendir, Maria Barrios, Davidson Barsky, Michael Bender, Liam Billingham, Joseph Binder, Julianna Bjorksten, Charles Borst, Lisa Borst, Emily Bryant-Alvarez, Eric Buechel, Sean Burns, Elena Saavedra Buckley, Jaquén Castellanos, Sophie Cavoulacos, Shannon Crawford, Benjamin De Roover, Florian Deroo, Jos Demme, Nina Eichacker, Ian Epstein, Fangtooth Books, Marcella Faustini, Connor Flanagan, Fernando Flores, George Fragopoulos, Lauren Frommer, Kyan Furlong, Jon Garelick, Demitri Garvey, Nathan Gelgud, Aaron Gensher, Leo Goldsmith, Akiva Gottlieb, Micah Gottlieb, Paul Granger, Harris Greenwood, Russell Harbaugh, Brandon Harris, Joan Hawkins, Carol Hayes, Jason Hellerstein, James Hubly, Justin Idlet, Matthew Johnson, Benjamin Joubert, Craig Keller, Colleen Kelsey, Glenn Kenny, Charlotta Kill, John Klacsmann, Daniel Kircher, Ryland Walker Knight, Jesse Kray, Quinn Kray, Aksel Kielland, Wiley Lawrence, Manuela Lazic, Nick LeBlanc,

Abby Lee, Jinnie Lee, Rose Lenehan, Lawrence Levi, Michael Lewy, James Long, Andrew Martin, Aiko Masubuchi, Amy Mathes, Celia Mattison, Tyler Maxin, Andrew McCarthy, Sean McCarthy, Steven Melone, Tom Mika, Jesse Milden, Andrew Miller, Michael Miller, Erica Moroz, Eric Muller, Morley Musick, Luke Olaf, George Olken, Eric Olson, Lucas Ospina, Maxwell Paparella, Kyle Paoletta, Asad Raza, John Reid, Megan Reid, Chris Richards, Vadim Rizov, Erica Rosenkranz, Johnny Ryan, Bijan S., Kat Sachs, Patrick Sandberg, Samantha Sartor, Ross Scarano, Martin Schauss, Aaron Schimberg, Chris Schlegel, Charlie Schneider, Andrew Schwartz, Cole Schwartz, Shaun Seneviratne, Milenko Skoknic, Danny Smight, Nora Smith, Henry Staley, Taylor Edelle Stuart, Dan Stuyck, Nick Tabor, Azra Thakur, Dave Tompkins, Andrea Torres, Robin Treadwell, Carlos Valladares, Alex Van Horn, Richard von Busack, Aimee Wall, Jeremy Wang-Iverson, Al Warren, Adam Webb, Carolyn Weaver, Claire Weissbluth, Andrew Williams, Sarah Winshall, and Jessica Winter

Apologies if I've missed anyone or misspelled your name.

A portion of *Last Week in End Times Cinema* was previously republished in issue 15 of the *Hoosac Journal* (June 2024).

Index